HEXHAM

history & guide

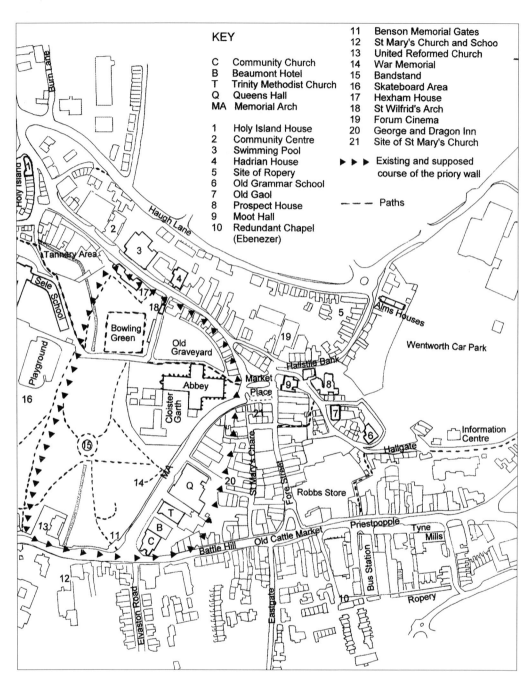

KEY

C — Community Church
B — Beaumont Hotel
T — Trinity Methodist Church
Q — Queens Hall
MA — Memorial Arch

1 Holy Island House
2 Community Centre
3 Swimming Pool
4 Hadrian House
5 Site of Ropery
6 Old Grammar School
7 Old Gaol
8 Prospect House
9 Moot Hall
10 Redundant Chapel (Ebenezer)

11 Benson Memorial Gates
12 St Mary's Church and Schoo
13 United Reformed Church
14 War Memorial
15 Bandstand
16 Skateboard Area
17 Hexham House
18 St Wilfrid's Arch
19 Forum Cinema
20 George and Dragon Inn
21 Site of St Mary's Church

▶ ▶ ▶ Existing and supposed course of the priory wall

– – – Paths

Map of the central area of Hexham. (Maureen Lazzari)

HEXHAM

history & guide

Stan Beckensall

TEMPUS

This book is dedicated to the memory of Anna Rossiter, who died of cancer on 13 May 2007 at the age of fifty-eight. She was a fine archivist and teacher, a great friend, and contributed enormously to the success of the Hexham Local History Society. May she rest in peace.

First published 2007

Tempus Publishing
Cirencester Road, Chalford,
Stroud, Gloucestershire, GL6 8PE
www.tempus-publishing.com

Tempus Publishing is an imprint of NPI Media Group

British Library Cataloguing in Publication Data.
A catalogue record for this book is available from the British Library.

ISBN 978 07524 4361 4

Typesetting and origination by NPI Media Group
Printed in Great Britain

Contents

Acknowledgements

I am grateful to all those who have researched the history of Hexham, and especially to those most recent contributors, Anna Rossiter, David and Ruth Jennings, and the late Tom Corfe. I am also indebted to Colin Dallison, Marjory Dallison, Neel Lever, Joan McCabe, Austin Wilson, and Pat Wilson for their work on the Cockshaw project, which enabled me to write the chapter on industry.

Most of the illustrations are my own; those produced by others are acknowledged in the text, and I should like to thank Maureen Lazzari, the Hexham Historic Partnership (P. Snowball), Peter Ryder, Matthew Hutchinson, Michaela Long, Colin Dallison, Birtley Aris and the Tynedale Museums Service. The Abbey plan appears by permission of the Rector, churchwardens and PCC of the Abbey, and the development plan of the Abbey is the work of past and present scholars.

I am grateful to people who have read part or all of the text, and offered their advice and comments: Matthew Hutchinson, Keith Young, Janet Goodridge, Anna Rossiter, Terry Robson, Rosalind Normandale and Lynn Turner

An Approach

When you visit a town for the first time or become aware that you have not really thought much about the place where you live (being so used to it that you take it for granted), where or when do you begin to understand it? Many will reach for the nearest guidebook so that they know what they are looking at. There is another way, simple in its idea, but perhaps more profitable in the long run: to walk around and really look hard at the town's buildings and open spaces. Not everyone will see the same thing; those who learn most from this may already be prepared through experience of other places, for 'chance favours the prepared mind'.

I begin with what can be seen and then go behind the façades to other resources such as old photographs and documents to try to understand how the town originated and developed, for history is about change rather than progress. Each building has a history from the time it was conceived, and its present use may be quite different from what was intended.

An invaluable handbook that readers may find not only fascinating but enlightening alongside this work is a book of old photographs and drawings that trace the history of Hexham visually with perceptive comments. This is *Hexham Remembered* by Hilary Kristensen and Colin Dallison (see Bibliography).

Chapter 1

The Town Centre and its Radiating Streets

Three distinct enclosures

The beginning is our modern starting point: what we can see today. The central point of the town is the Market Place. The photograph helps us to see it in relationship to its immediate surroundings, but if you sit on one of the seats there, stand, or walk around, you will soon see what part different building materials play. The Abbey's east end is made of relatively new, precisely-cut light sandstone, but its windows echo an Early English pointed style ('lancet') that exists in an older version to the north and south. The building is now surrounded by new sandstone slab paving. Roads meet at the Market Place, where opposite the Abbey is an impressively large fortified tower built of aged sandstone. Defensive, you will conclude, with arches leading through it to another massive tower that was a purpose-built gaol. So at once we see that defence, a power-base, punishment and religion are represented in the Market Place.

The buildings that face the Market Place are a mixture of brick and stone. As though to highlight the Abbey's importance, some have pointed arches, an echo of a 'church' style. Many look like large town houses with shops inserted. There is a cinema (The Forum) and a Wetherspoon's on the corner of a small road running down the hill towards the river. An Indian restaurant overhangs a jeweller's like some medieval town building with protruding joists on Market Street, where another road squeezes through a gap to run down to the Tyne.

To the south, a narrow passage with an old arch leads to another narrow street called St Mary's Chare, or Back Street, and parallel to it is Fore Street, now the main shopping road. Between the two exits on the south is an open building with a roof supported by rounded pillars, known as 'The Shambles', opposite a drinking fountain surmounted by a gold cross.

More will be said about these features, but we have started with a nucleus, a junction of small roads. If we look more closely at the west wall of the Moothall before we leave, we will see that several pieces of sandstone have been taken out in an ascending pattern, and that one arch support appears to have been 'shaved'. Such clues remind us of the changes in use that buildings may have over time, and old photographs might tell us what and how.

A question that arises is why this nucleus of buildings and roads occupies this site. Towns don't just appear by accident. If you examine any hole in the road when work is being done, or a building site, you will see that the town is built on large rounded pebbles and small boulders, sand and clay. This is glacial material from the last Ice Age, dumped as the glaciers retreated. A bird's-eye view, confirmed by walking around the site, shows that some streams flow as tributaries into the River Tyne. To the north, on either side of the river, is alluvium, silt deposited by water, providing a fertile soil. The descent to the river from the Market Place or past the Old Gaol to the Wentworth car park and the view of Hexham

The Abbey is central, with the Sele grassland surrounded by trees. To the left is the road from Corbridge, here called Battle Hill and Hencotes. To the right are Haugh Lane and Eilansgate, with an industrial/retail area to the right. Between these roads is the historic centre of Hexham, with the Moothall and Old Gaol at the bottom.

The Market Place reconstruction panel. (Courtesy of Hexham Historic Partnership)

The Old Gaol.

The west wall of the Moothall.

Market Place during the Hexham
Abbey Festival, north side.

The Forum Cinema and Wetherspoon's today.

Two hotels occupied the same site. A fire is being extinguished. The buildings on the right were demolished in the 1950s.

The Moothall arch through to the Market Place.

from the Tyne shows that the town is based on a dissected platform, high above the river flood-level, reasonably well-drained, served by springs and streams, with level areas and steep smaller valleys. Of crucial importance is the large bridge over the river, and the site of a fording-place (colour 1,2,3,4).

The ridges flanking the valley on both sides are pronounced and have provided suitable routes for trackways, linked to the town itself. A walk west and south-west from the Abbey takes you into beautiful parkland, called the Abbey Grounds, and high above this is the open, tree-encircled hill called the Sele (or Seal), overlooking the river to the north and flanked by two streams on the east and west. Although it is obvious that much building has filled the town centre and outskirts, these open spaces have been untouched, except to make them more beautiful. There is a reason why they have escaped development and the modern land-grab, which we will discover later

The south of the town has a fairly straight road running from Corbridge past the General Hospital in the east and has such intriguing names as Priestpopple and Battle Hill, with an offshoot road called Eastgate. This is a road of finely-built banks, which one might expect in an important market town, and of inns, hotels, restaurants, charity shops, house agents and some small shops struggling against giant retailers. Some of the buildings are elegant, others boringly functional, and that there is a decrepit area housing the bus station is perhaps a comment on the neglect of public transport, not a hopeful sign for an alternative to the car.

So far this account and illustrations are a taster, but it is an essential basis on which to build what is to follow. Everything so far can be seen. The whys and wherefores demand a different approach.

An enclosure for worship: The Abbey

The Abbey is a constant factor in the history of Hexham from its beginning, so I have chosen to introduce different aspects of the building throughout this chapter. Its changes are linked to changes in the development of the town.

The Abbey, so dominant in size and position, is the oldest known foundation in the town. The east end, which faces the Market Place, speaks of rebuilding, and not only can you see a join marking the difference between new and old stone as you move west but also the roof line rises on the newer part. Further west the transepts jut out, making the building cross-shaped. A close look at stone on the north wall shows a blocked-up low doorway which was probably used during building work, but further west at the transept is new stone that blocks a removed doorway that threatened to weaken the whole of the north transept wall. At the end of the transept is an open space with stone coffins leaning against the nave wall, grass, a few more recent gravestones, and what is clearly a very new nave built on the foundations of something older. The graves and a raised, walled area to the north of this show where the town cemetery used to be, with a few 'token' grave slabs left to mark it. The west end of the building shows the same ancient foundation and door, backing on to space formed by walls and buildings, one of which has the Carnaby coat of arms. As we shall see, one member benefited from the Dissolution and turned part of the Abbey buildings into a house for himself.

To the south, via a passage that has an arch leading into the 'Monastic Workshop', are the cloisters, a large grassed area with the modern nave on an older foundation that includes stone tombs inserted into the wall, and an early range of church buildings to the east with stone seats in recessed arches – the original cloister wall, dated by the style of the arches. Opposite is more rebuilding, with some fragments of wash basins displayed to remind us that here the canons washed before meals. From the open north end a whole range of buildings has been removed. A reconstruction drawing shows what the area might have looked like at an earlier stage in its history.

The bridge (1793), with resident black-headed gulls.

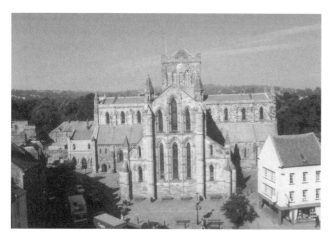

The Abbey from the Moothall.

The Abbey north wall.

The arms of Sir Reynold Carnaby (1537).

Display panel: the cloister garth. (Courtesy of Hexham Historic Partnership)

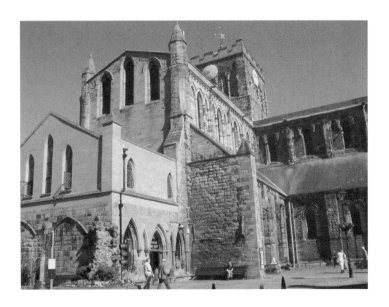

The Abbey from the south.

The transept is extended into a building topped by a new choir school, its new stone beginning to blend in with the rest of the building, and a passage ('The Slype') leads back to where we started, this time over newly laid flagstones.

From even this brief tour, some of the Abbey's early and recent history is apparent in the structure, but the depth of its history must be experienced now from the inside. You enter through a doorway into a passage which connected the cloisters with the burial ground and the Chapter House (where business was conducted). A wonderful eruption of arches greets you in the south transept.

We will have time to look for all the things that make this building so interesting, but it is not a museum. That is why it has such atmosphere, when one considers the time taken to bring it from its Anglo-Saxon roots to the present.

The seventh-century crypt is a most remarkable construction, dating the foundation of the great building that was to rise above it, to fall, to be rebuilt and extended. It is the heart of St Wilfrid's church, and we will go down the ancient stone steps into its dimly-lit vaults and corridors. For those who have visited Roman sites on Hadrian's Wall there is something at once familiar in the masonry and the way the blocks of stone are shaped and gouged, and Roman decoration becomes more and more obvious as one examines each stone.

There are two corridors on either side of a vault, with the remains of steps leading from the east above, all narrow, constricted, awesome. Think of pilgrims coming down one stairway, passing the vault with relics on display, and then climbing another stair to reach the ground floor again. It is not difficult to imagine people packed into this small space, shuffling through, as though on a conveyor belt of

devotees, controlled, urged on by officials. Today two entrances are sealed off. If we have time, an examination of the stonework will reveal not only decoration, but Roman inscriptions, one defaced deliberately in Roman times, and traces of plaster on the walls. It has recently been shown from a detailed recording of all these stones that many come from a recently-excavated bridge at Coria (Corbridge). If you were an Anglo-Saxon mason looking for building material, what better place than an abandoned Roman fort or other building, where the work of quarrying and shaping had been done for you?

There has been speculation about whether the Romans had some sort of settlement in Hexham, but there is no evidence for this. Here the Roman stone was brought from Coria, possibly by road to the south of the river, or, more unlikely, by rafts along the river itself. Even a

The crypt (Birtley Aris).

Reused Roman stone in the crypt.

Roman sculpted stone displayed in the nave.

geophysical scan of the Abbey Grounds and bowling green did not locate a supposed Roman fort; although the Romans would no doubt have used the area, their main lines were to the north, along the old Antonine frontier (the 'Stane Gate', the stone road) and, later, the Hadrian's Wall area.

So what might have been here before the time of the Romans? We have no buildings of the prehistoric period. What was standing on this site when Wilfrid chose it to build his monastery? Perhaps there is one clue in the name 'Hexham'.

The study of names is very important. As the older settlements are documented in this way, they may tell us who settled there, what kind of land it was and what grew there, which animals were prominent, and many other things. Hexham is not easy to understand, especially when we look at its earliest form: *Ecclesia Hagustaldensis*. After that, its name was changed many times, with copies made of copies. We know that the region where the House of the Lord was built was given to Wilfrid by Queen Aethelthryth (or Etheldreda) in the early 670s, in honour of St Andrew. It would have been in a region with sufficient income to sustain it, and would have drawn on other income further afield. Here the wealth would have come from arable farming, fishing, and stock-rearing.

The land belonged to the *hagustald*, who in Anglo-Saxon society was the younger son of a person of some importance who could not inherit land from his father. Instead he had to go out to find some for himself. A *haga* is a hedge used for enclosure. The pronunciation may have become 'hestald'.

The second element in the name (ea), usually translated as 'river', may mean an island; not necessarily an island in a river, but a detached piece of land, and there are many possibilities of land between rivers, streams or marshes. A 'ham' is a common element given to a settlement. So we do not have to think of Wilfrid building his church in a wilderness. As with so many other places within the Roman Wall 'corridor', not quite so much attention has been given to the people living here before more powerful people moved in to take control. I have wondered what the impact of such an important project as the building of a church that was to become known as the greatest north of the Alps and the development of a town around it would have made on local people. I speculated about this in a poem, which is not historical truth, but imagination that fits what little we know:

The Forerunners

Out of the river mist we saw our landing site,
As wild geese broke the silence with their hurried flight.
A curling thread of woodsmoke shimmered from a dark, low roof,
Carrying a scent of fragrant cooking drifting towards fields
Won from woodland clearings and from burnt-out scrub.

We hauled our raft ashore and toiled along the track
That led from riverbank to settlement.
Rough farmers stumbled down the slope to meet with us,
Fingering their spades and hoes in challenge to our right.

'We speak for Etheldreda, Queen, and for your new lord Wilfrid.'

Such words had their effect; there was no one to dare
The voicing of a disagreement with the power of Church and State.
They knew the limitations of their role in life.
Theirs to plough, to till, to sow, to reap the harvest of their toil;
Theirs to secure the boundaries of fields,
To keep their beasts from harm in pastures close to home;
Theirs to protect their wives and bairns;
Theirs to obey, or break out in a rage
When what they built up, what they loved
Was doomed or under threat.

'We come in peace. We bring good news.'

Could any news from that far land of Church and State be good?

'You have a chance to walk with God, to build His temple in this place.'

We had already made a choice of land to build our church:
There on the hill, flanked by the streams that fed the Tyne.

'Hagustaldensis, now famous in the eyes of men
Is where you share the glory and the power.'

That's what we told them, yet we knew
What all the coming changes meant to them:
A higher price for food, a ready market close at hand,
Work in the quarries, work to fashion stone,
Work with timber, jobs for all at home.

They wanted to know more; we squatted in their dismal huts,
Stared at by finger-sucking bairns
And drank the proffered, bitter brew.
We told them of the plans, the wondrous transformation of their land,
Of Wilfrid's vision of the rising church
To meet God in the clouds of Hexham's skies.
We offered gifts, for we had come prepared
And knew before we left that soon from miles around
The hunters and the herdsmen, farmers, those with skill
Would make their way from hills and woods and fields
To do God's work, and benefit themselves.

How could such a building have disappeared? Archaeology does not tell us much, although there have been opportunities to look below the surface. Violence and insecurity played their parts, and one poignant sign of this is that someone buried over 8,000 Anglo-Saxon coins in a bronze bucket, not to be found until the nineteenth century by a gravedigger. The church, no longer a cathedral, continued to be used, despite Viking incursions and internal strife. One has only to look at the bishops depicted in paintings on wood in the Abbey and the list of incumbents to see that there was a continuation of its role as a church. This, however, had to be supported by civil power in turbulent times, for the Church could not be a law unto itself.

The early history of the Church was part of the 'Golden Age of Northumbria' – that creative, exciting time that produced conversions to Christianity, learning and masterpieces such as the Lindisfarne Gospels. No matter how little we know about the fortunes of the Priory, we can be sure that the next major event in its history was the coming of the Normans, and the arrival of the first Augustinian Canons, which resulted in such rebuilding that the last traces of the cathedral disappeared.

If you turn your attention to the scattered pieces of sculpture that are preserved in the Abbey, the oldest are Roman, and after that, the Anglian sculptures, especially crosses. The photograph shows a copy of the Gospels on the Frith stool which dates from the foundation of the cathedral, but which has been moved around, dropped, cracked, and badly repaired.

Norman-style rounded arches gave way as fashions changed to the pointed 'Gothic' arch. In the choir under a trapdoor is the east end of a church later than the Saxon cathedral: a rounded apse. Like that at Holy Island in the same period, this was demolished to make way for an extension of the building to the east, joining on to and assimilating a small chapel.

The facsimile Lindisfarne Gospels displayed on the Frith Stool.

An Anglian 'rosette' from an earlier building on display in the nave.

Religion and secular power have always been inter-dependent. Wilfrid, later to be elevated as a saint, was recruited from an upper-class family that produced wealthy and educated children, who had powers beyond being clergy. As 'clerics' they could read, write and administer. Bishops had powers equal to those of princes; York and Durham were great centres of such power, both involved in running Hexham at different times. We shall return to the Abbey to see more of its history and use, but the focus shifts back to the Market Place to show clear signs of this power.

An enclosure for commerce: the Market Place

The histories of town and Abbey are inextricably linked. The town is there because a monastery was built. The Moothall across the Market Place was an administrative centre, a gateway into a probable walled enclosure that housed other buildings, including the early gaol. We see Hexham occupying a site which probably had a small population, central to a 'Golden Age' of Christianity and learning with a world-famous reputation and a strong missionary zeal.

The Priory was both of the town and separate from it. You may notice in your tour that parts of a high stone wall survive, best seen at the back of the Queen's Hall to the rear of a marvellously restored seventeenth-century 'courtyard' inn, 'The George and Dragon'. It can be traced all round the Abbey Grounds, and is breached in Market Street by an early round-arched gatehouse that had rooms built above it. Walls keep people in as well as out, so the canons' area was defined clearly. Today the changes have been such that town and Abbey are no longer separated even by grass and a low 'token' wall, but the paving comes right up to the walls, where seats have been added. It is a clear statement about access and relationships.

So far many of these changes are visible, but to appreciate fully the ways things can change, look at the painting of a scene in the Market Place by Henry Perlee Parker around 1820 in the colour section (colour 5). The painting shows a similar grouping to one entitled '1st or King's Dragoon Guards Shifting their Luggage near St Nicholas' church, Newcastle'. It is the background that differs, and this tells us much about what Hexham looked like about 200 years ago, information which is confirmed with added detail by other artists such as Carmichael. Compare this with the same viewpoint today; what is at once obvious is the crowding of buildings at the east end of the Abbey, a different east end with a rose window and pinnacles, and a stone 'pant' (source of water) in one corner. The picture was a recent discovery and is now in the Abbey office. The Newcastle scene was bought by Lord Lonsdale of Lowther Castle, Cumbria. The Market Place remains in part an open space, but more hemmed in by buildings.

This drawing turns attention to the east, where again buildings crowd another ancient structure, the Moothall. Now that some of these buildings have been removed (in the early 1950s) you can see where the wall of the hall has been used to support them. The lovely inn, 'The White Horse', shown in some of the early pictures on the south side of the hall, has been replaced by another stone-fronted building (colour 6).

The drawing shows the buildings clustered against the Abbey, and a carnival atmosphere. The activity of people in these pictures shows the importance of Hexham as a market, for the town is in a large agricultural area, the market of which would attract cattle and sheep for sale and slaughter, and all sorts of other goods. The animals, slaughtered within the town, would be skinned. Their skins would then be traded, becoming part of a flourishing leather-making industry. With industry and trade came itinerant labour, and pressure on housing and other facilities, another strand in the story that will be taken up later. We shall see too how place names themselves are evidence of such activities: Glovers' Place, Tannery Row and The Skinners' Arms are evocative, for example.

An enclosure for administration

The Moothall ('moot' being a meeting-place) is one of two visible defensive towers, separated from the walled Priory, occupying a piece of levelled ground that slopes steeply away from the town centre. This area may be thought of as a single complex, with its entrance through the hall gateways, leading from the Market Place. The two towers have been thoroughly investigated architecturally by Peter Ryder (1994 Ryder) within an enclosure often referred to as 'the Archbishop's enclosure', which Peter believes to have been walled. The Moothall is also written as 'Moot Hall', but the Tynedale Museums prefer it to be one word, out of respect to the Lockhart family who called it this when they owned it and the gaol. Without them, the buildings would not now be open to the public, so I am happy to write it this way.

As you pass through the vaulted entrance of the Moothall, with its stone staircase at the back giving access to the tower, ahead of you is a curious concoction of different styles known as Prospect House,

Remains of the Priory wall behind 'The George and Dragon'.

The mid-twelfth-century gateway through the Priory wall.

The east Market Place in the early nineteenth century. The White Horse Inn lies to the right of the Moothall arch, and a block of brick buildings has been constructed against its other wall. The 'pant', a communal source of water, was demolished after the Public Health report of 1853.

The west, before drastic changes to remove buildings attached to the east end of the Abbey. There is an air of carnival about the scene. The 'Catherine wheel' window was removed along with the east end, and all the buildings packed against the Abbey were demolished.

Prospect House.

now the Tynedale District Council offices, which overlooks the industrial expansion along the river. Although it has stone in its structure, modern, it is mainly built with an attractive red brick, and is separated from the Old Gaol on one side by a narrow lane leading to the east edge of the enclosure. To the north of Prospect House, buildings include one with tiled Masonic symbols. Below this, on Hallstile, the steep road leading to the river, on the right-hand side is a substantial vaulted cellar that may belong to a tower or some other stone building on the flank of the enclosure, with signs of older walls at the base of a modern wall that continues around the enclosure.

The Old Gaol has been extensively refashioned inside and pointed outside recently, but the outer stonework, as you can see, is substantially unchanged. With its coursed sandstone blocks of varying size and thickness, it is clearly meant to be a stronghold, though not a castle. Its slightly jutting-out flat roof was meant to support an overhanging platform. The two towers and possible line of an enclosure wall were probably accompanied by other buildings such as stables and lodgings. This area became a base

A vaulted cellar in Hallstile, possibly in part of an enclosure wall.

for administration by the Archbishop of York, confirmed later by King Henry I, and carried out by a bailiff and his justices. In time it was thought necessary to build a gaol 'in which prisoners may be incarcerated and securely guarded, the expenses of which were to be paid out of the revenues of the shire', as a letter from the Archbishop to Thomas Fox (the 'receiver' of Hexham) stated in 1330. The building was opened in 1333, and supplied with chains, manacles and a gaoler (who was also a barber). There is documentary evidence that other buildings at the same time were crumbling, including the predecessor of the Moothall (the present one dates to about 1400). One hundred years later one learns that they were both in decay, a major problem with large buildings of this type which cost so much to maintain; documents are full of complaints of people not having enough money to repair Border defences, for example.

This brief background may be considered when you view the two towers more closely. Now for some more detail.

The Moothall

The hall is built as a rectangle or block of stone three storeys high with two tall towers at the south end built over vaults, making the ground plan T-shaped. The cellar which supports the building is now used for art exhibitions. The ground floor, reached by a stone staircase at the back of the building, is a rectangle smaller than the other floors, now housing a museum, and with a spiral staircase in the south-east corner, leading to the floors above and to the flat roof. As with other rooms, artificial stone has been used in its refurbishing, and some larger windows inserted. The buttress to the north of the outside staircase was also a garderobe (lavatory). Above that, the second floor, called the Lockhart Room and used for civic functions, dance classes and entertainment, has an impressive large fireplace and some good timbers. The facing stone is artificial and no window is original. Above this room, the roof consists of eight bays, made from ancient timber. The corbels that jut out would have been for an overhanging platform.

A drawing of the Moothall on a display panel outside Prospect House. (Courtesy of Hexham Historic Partnership)

The Moothall.

The two south towers had three rooms above the arches that span the entrance from the Market Place. All have single small windows, some now blocked. A stone stair on the outside goes up to the roof, and the larger eastern tower also has an internal spiral staircase. The most important room has a two-light window with pointed heads, and this may have been the residence for the Archbishop's bailiff, as the building was used as a courtroom. The bailiff would have had a suite of rooms, one with a stone bowl, and they would have been much lighter than the others. The top rooms of the towers may have been for watchmen, who could get onto the roof easily. The oldest part of this building of about 1400 is best seen in an unrestored state on the south side. By the eighteenth century the south and east parts had been used as a wall for other buildings, with a clock set in a large diamond-shaped wooden panel. These buildings were demolished in 1951, with no record kept, and a major restoration in 1977 was followed by more recent refurbishing.

The Old Gaol

The Old Gaol is still referred to as 'The Manor Office', its later function. It is a rectangular three-storey stone block, originally with an overhanging parapet supported by corbels. The stone is roughly square, in courses, mostly small, with occasional large ones that may have been reused from elsewhere. The dungeons are barrel-vaulted, roughly square, one of the 'oubliette' type, a term coming from a French word to show that the prisoners there were forgotten. The first floor has three rooms formed by inserting transverse walls, with few old features. The second floor, where the masonry changes to worn, roughly-squared stones, has some with Roman-style diagonal tooling, seen on all the outside walls. One room has two original fireplaces. The roof is recent, mid-nineteenth century, with chimney stacks.

New access to the entrance and the upper rooms by lift, and its refurbishment, are an investment to enhance it as a Border Museum, but outside it hasn't changed much from the fourteenth century, when some rooms equipped with garderobes, fireplaces and light were for the gaoler's use. There is little evidence of change until the late eighteenth or early nineteenth century. Last used as a gaol in 1824, it was converted to a Manor Office. Later that century the dungeon was discovered and cleaned out. It became the Middle March Museum of Border History in late 1970.

So what we have in this precinct are strongly-built administrative buildings firmly dominated by York, likely to have been enclosed all round with a wall, the main entrance being from the Market Place, and including many other buildings later to be built over. One such building is the Old Grammar School of 1684, in use as council offices. It may be difficult to reconstruct this precinct with any certainty, but the term 'Hexham Castle' for its use is incorrect. If any building work is done here later, providing an opportunity to look under the surface, more information will come from careful study and archaeology. In the past, Hexham has not been very good at that, but, hopefully, times have changed.

What about the time gap?

As these pieces of the jigsaw puzzle of Hexham's early history fall into place, from Anglian times or even earlier to the present, it is clear that there are some gaps; there are many things we should like to know, but have no material. Although documents are so important in finding out what happened in history (bearing in mind that these can be biased, distorted, and fragmentary as well), our only chance comes from archaeology. Again, it is back to the Abbey to investigate this, as the earliest existing monument that we have. If we bear in mind that the time gap between Saxon and Norman was as much as 400 years, which alone is a huge gap to fill – what can we now add?

A certainty is that the earlier buildings where the Abbey now stands were re-founded as an Augustinian Priory. Not only do documents show this, but also remains of that earlier building have been found or incorporated in the present Abbey. An example of recent excavations came in 1984 when the building we now know as the gift shop, once the Chapter House vestibule of the Priory (a place where administrative and other issues were dealt with), was being created from the ruins of the old. If you view this building from the cloisters, you are looking at a thirteenth-century wall (see Appendix 1).

At the time when the Normans conquered the North, Eilaf was the priest at Hexham, and it was his decision not to become a monk when Durham became a Benedictine Priory in 1083 that led Hexham to become part of the Archbishopric of York, the new Priory being founded by the Augustinians in 1113. Whilst it was being built, there must have been many temporary buildings scattered around, many probably in the open space of the cloister area. Once the work went ahead we would have seen a

The Old Gaol. (Courtesy of Hexham Historic Partnership)

East cloister wall.

building go up like that on the plan, all its axes on the same alignment as the modern Abbey and the pre-Conquest building. All this was walled. Later, in the late twelfth or thirteenth century, the cloister was enlarged to what we see today.

Documents provide another possibility for the early history of the Hexham church: that Wilfrid in fact built three churches there. Whereas it is possible that his second was a little chapel at the east end of his cathedral, to be swallowed up in later building work, his church of St Mary may well be under a later church of that name, the more recent with its foundations now visible in the cellar of shops bordering the market on the south. The story goes that he was facing death when on the Continent and vowed that if he could be spared he would build a church to honour Mary. His other two were dedicated to male saints. Whether this church still lies underneath the accumulation of old and modern buildings is not known, despite hopeful attempts to find it after two recent fires in those buildings.

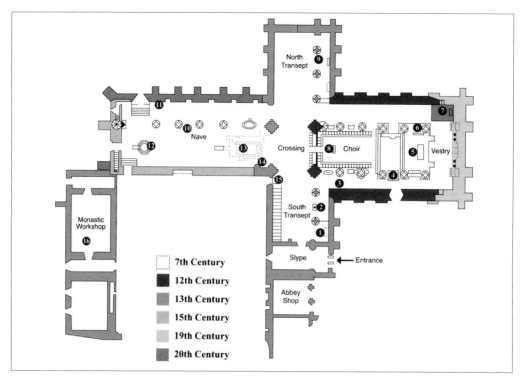

Plan of the Abbey. Of particular interest are: 1. Etheldreda chapel; 2. Saxon crosses; 3. The chalice; 4. The Ogle Chantry; 5. High Altar; 6. Leschman's chantry; 7. Wilfrid's chapel and the Passion paintings; 8. Frith stool; 11. Ancient sculpture; 12. Font; 13. Crypt; 14. The Millennium tapestry 15. Night stair. (Courtesy of the Rector, churchwardens and PCC of Hexham Abbey)

Underneath the market and pavements

It is possible that the church of St Mary had its own burial ground to the south, although it is very unlikely that it would have encroached on the market area. An opportunity came for some extensive archaeological observation and excavation quite by chance, and it was most fortunate that I had taken early retirement when the opportunity arose.

I began this book with the central position of the Market Place, but was it always like that, or were there buildings on it? This is an important question that the laying of new Telecom pipes and cables in 1990 was able to answer. There was no 'watching brief' when this work was carried out, but I saw how necessary this was and did it myself out of interest. It meant recording sections in the neatly-dug trenches across the Market Place, and soon it was clear that below the tarmac and its shallow foundation was a layer of vertically-set light-coloured sandstones: the old Market Place surface, seen in the painting (colour 5). Where the roads left the Market Place, this surface stopped; there was no sign of any building foundations and the 'natural' was reached in some places.

The next phase was quite startling, as the machines began to unearth burials and scattered bone under the pavement to the south of the Abbey chancel aisle. Again, there was no official watching brief, but with the aid of local archaeologists, a GP and a dental pathologist, I was able to record the remains *in situ*, remove all the loose bones for forensic examination at the RVI in Newcastle, and arrange for the sealing in of those exposed in the trenches. This was a great moment; as the curate read a prayer for the

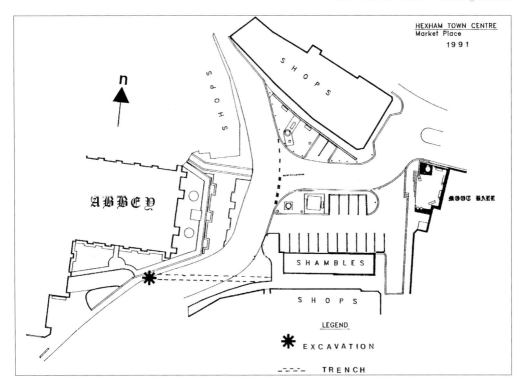

The 1990 excavation site at the end of a trench running from the Market Place.

dead over the trench, the workmen and I stood by with heads bowed. Then the trench was filled with sand, wire netting and cement so that no more damage could be done to the skeletons. You walk over this area when you approach the Slype entrance and the Abbey gift shop.

There remained the fragments of the skeletons of many canons, all of which were meticulously examined, some with x-rays, in laboratories, and a picture given of their state of health, age, state of their teeth (and diet), among other things. All the bones were to be returned to the Abbey, as we wished to rebury them with dignity. Whether you believe that bones matter or not, the point is that these bodies had been buried with care, according to a belief, and we respected that. So, one evening after Sunday evensong, the congregation and choir moved to the north transept, a small section of the floor having been excavated to receive the bones, and they were reburied to the singing of a *Nunc Dimittis*. Much has been written about what archaeologists should do about the remains they excavate, and I was totally satisfied that we had brought this matter to a proper conclusion, and the BBC's *Look North* allowed others to share the moment in a beautifully produced programme.

The burials had an interesting story to tell. It may have been assumed that the earliest burials belonged to the time of Wilfrid's cathedral, but no one was sure where the burial ground was. The trench section showed clearly that the lower skeletons, uncoffined, were buried on their sides, faces to the south, whereas the others, though mixed up as a result of the same ground being used again and disturbed for building, included one which lay stretched out on its back, aligned east-west. This pattern of the later burials was to be confirmed.

By now this sensitive area was to be carefully monitored when it was decided to repave the area to the south and east of the Abbey with sandstone slabs. These required a shallow foundation, but such a foundation could disturb more burials. Unfortunately, a survey of the area failed to locate what later turned out to be an extensive series of burials, mainly of canons lying on their backs, arms crossed over the pelvis, or over their chests, some covered with slabs of the types still displayed in the Abbey with the canons' names. The machines had already been allowed to begin the removal of the top layer when this was discovered, but the site became one that demanded that the Newcastle Archaeological Practice should excavate it. This was done to a good standard, and not only were the burials recovered and bagged when they were in the way of foundation material but the remains of a medieval chapel and a nineteenth-century boiler house were found too.

Beaumont Street, which skirts the Abbey to the south, had been cut through the cemetery and Abbey grounds in the nineteenth century, with the removal and dumping of many bones. John Dobson's plan for the reconstruction of the east face of the Abbey involved further disturbance of this cemetery, and a charnel pit was made there for the bones.

When the second excavations had finished, the bones were brought back to the Abbey from the laboratory for reburial. This time the number was greater, and a new grave had to be dug for them. This too proved interesting, for I chose a place in the north transept close to the west wall where there were signs in the paving that a heating duct had once run through. These ducts, which destroyed a great deal of archaeology when they were laid in the nineteenth century, were connected to the furnace site on the south side of the Abbey, forming a kind of hypocaust system rather like that in Roman buildings on the Wall. As churches were greatly favoured for burials, there were many under the floors, and there are reports of these being unceremoniously dug out and their contents dumped. Indeed, the building of Beaumont Street in the late nineteenth century led to one commentator saying that skeletons were seen, 'peering from almost every square foot of earth'.

On one occasion in the 1970s part of the floor of the transept caved in, and during rebuilding, there were many bones found as well as graves and vaulted tunnels. The scientific excavation of the new grave revealed one of these heating ducts made of stone and brick, packed with dark soil, pieces of nineteenth-century pottery and bits of coal, but the space so formed made an ideal grave for the reburial service. This time the congregation was joined by English Heritage officials and a Sikh family, the father of whom was working on DNA for UNESCO, and had been given small samples for his research. The bones are under the floor, bagged in plastic and labelled, having been given more reverential treatment than thousands of others in this building. Thus recent excavations have added a little more to an understanding of the history of this site, and the lesson learnt is that the Abbey is such an important and sensitive building that any building work in future must be very carefully monitored, and opportunities taken to learn more from disturbances.

The story of what happened to the east end of the Abbey demonstrates how awful things can be. Once there was a row of chapels behind the high altar (as at Durham Cathedral) that became so completely encased in domestic buildings that they could no longer be seen. We have an early photograph of them, and the oil painting shows the Abbey rising behind them with a rose or 'Catherine wheel' window (colour 5). In 1823 they were known as 'the old school' and this part of the Abbey may have been so-used for a while. Whether or not buildings had been filling in the space between the Priory and its wall before the Dissolution is not known, although there were buildings there in the seventeenth century. The 'school' itself was maintained by payments to traders from 1722-1739 who re-glazed its windows. Perhaps this was an early grammar school. John Dobson was responsible for the final act of destruction of these chapels. In 1828 the rose window seen in the pictures had fallen in; he was annoyed that it was

The 1993 excavations: grass, soil and rubble have been stripped off, revealing the walls of a chapel broken by pipes, its buttress at the top right. (Peter Ryder)

restored, as he wanted it replaced with pointed arches. In 1858 he was given the chance to do what he wanted to the hated 'Catherine wheel', although an early public meeting in the Moothall had wanted the chapels to be restored in all their glory, free of clutter. Dobson's scheme, the result of which we see today, won in the end, and that was a minor tragedy for Hexham.

Other changes to the Abbey surroundings culminated in the recent 'floorscaping' with sandstone paving. The ground to the south, south-east and east of the transept and chancel had been used for gardens and buildings, the latter crowding the way into the Abbey and being responsible for dirt and bad smells. Rawlinson singled the area out for comment and had a plan drawn of these buildings, so there is no doubt how awful it must have been.

By 1859 all this clutter had gone when William Blackett Beaumont bought the land and buildings and demolished them, so the church stood alone until Beaumont Street was built through the grounds to the south. We have seen that there was a furnace house on the site that had disturbed many burials in 1830. Sadly, this led to other disturbances in the building too, as the channels were 120ft long, 6ft wide and 5ft deep. An article in *The Builder* of 1850 reports how burials inside were disturbed, skeletons being wheeled out openly, and coffin lids of all periods being used to cover the vents. The furnace house too was demolished by 1859, its location being confirmed in the 1990s excavations, along with the discovery of the medieval chapel.

The building of Beaumont Street was a major upheaval, as we see from old photographs, not only of the cemetery but of the Chapter House, dormitory, undercroft and possibly the infirmary. It is clear from what remains how much has been chopped off, and reconstruction drawings aim at showing what it might have looked like before these drastic changes. At that time not much notice was taken of the

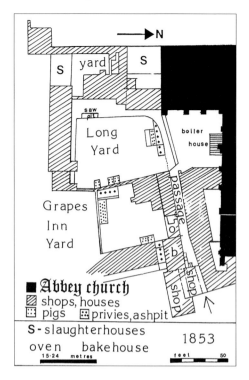

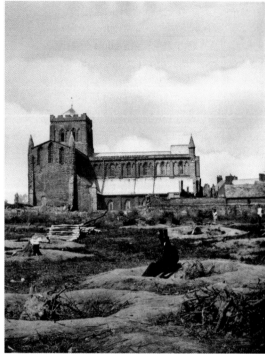

Above left: The buildings clustered round the Abbey in 1853, according to the Public Health report. The boiler house later proved to be in the top right-hand corner, and the hatched area is the medieval chapel base.

Above right: The building of Beaumont Street: in preparation for this, the Abbey grounds have been torn apart (Tynedale Museums Service).

archaeology, and this has been part of Hexham's story. What we are left with today is a town centre that has reached the Abbey walls, that has swept away the insanitary and unsightly buildings as well as destroying some fine ones (colour 29).

The history of the Abbey, reflected in its contents

To end this section on the town centre, the continuity of the Abbey's history is largely visual, so we will go inside again. If you enter from the south, the usual way, you are in the south transept, one arm of the cross jutting out to the south. I offer a poem of the impact of this on the senses:

Hexham Abbey: Candlelight

Enter. You meet prayer-soaked stone
Invested with soft light, broken by stained glass.
You meet wood, warmed with time,
Darkened by caring, polished by use.
You meet images in paint:

Hollow-eyed Death, presiding over
The dance of the feckless and unsuspecting.
Here are lines of bishops and saints
Stretching in strips, with snatches of story.

Time spins and spirals all in one blend.
Brittle fragments of the Empire that was Rome,
Bundled Gothic pillars, black-edged in strong sunshine shafts,
An order of mind transformed to order by hands
That wield chisel and mallet.
Arches glimpsed through arches,
Soaring out of sight, upwards,
Light lingering on light.
Shadows shifting, corners hiding.

Listen now.
Bass from deep-throated organ pipes
Rends the foundations on which arches lie.
Light notes float among the curves
And thread among patterned stones.
Add candlelight: the melting shapes
Make tableaux of their own,
White stalactites, winged angels,
Birth and crucifixion all in one.
The soft, light touch of candle flame
Strokes the arch's throat, bends pillars inward.
Golden clerestory holds its shadows on a gentler rein,
And human faces are transformed
By wonder and an inner light.
All things conspire to lift the soul above the earth
From which this Abbey grows.
The tiny parts fail by themselves to move;
The way they blend
Disturbs us to the roots.

There is an immediate contrast, for the wall to the right has arches and an aisle, but the left has a stair rising to a higher platform against a wall that is punctured at its base by a blocked arch to the cloisters, covered by a dramatic memorial to the Roman standard-bearer, Flavinus.

This was probably brought from Corbridge with other building material and was buried by the Augustinian canons face upwards in the foundations of the east range of the cloister. It was found during an investigation by C.C. Hodges of the floor of the Slype. He moved it to its present position. It is a very impressive memorial, complete with an inscription which tells us that he was in Candidus's troop of the Ala Petriana, a Petrian cavalry unit. He died at the age of twenty-five. Like many others of its kind it shows the Roman contempt for the defeated hairy Britunculus, the local Brit, being trampled under the horse's hooves, wielding his inadequate short sword. He died sometime just before the end of the first century AD.

The night stair and west wall.

He, of course, belongs to a period hundreds of years before Wilfrid built his church, but the memorial stands at the foot of the rare night stair, which linked the chancel with the canons' sleeping quarters. Here we can appreciate that the canons used the stair to attend their many acts of worship – seven times in the day and night. The Choir preserves some of the seats, known as misericords, where they could rest their backsides whilst giving the appearance of standing, for a life of prayer was hard. The place where they entered the building that contained their dormitory is now the doorway to the choir school, and to the east of that door is an older door leading to the treasury, with barred windows still in place.

The right side with the aisle and arches has some fine but poorly displayed painted panels at floor level. Each section is devoted to a bishop or other eminent ecclesiastic, all part of the remarkable survivals of paintings on wood throughout the Abbey belonging to the fifteenth century, much later than the stonework that houses them. The chapel here is devoted to Etheldreda, who had given land and income for the building of Wilfrid's church.

At a higher level, above the arches that spring from clustered shafts at the second level, containing arches within arches, there are more recently painted panels, one of a rather characterless angel which has been inappropriately adopted as a logo for a vibrant annual Abbey Festival of the Arts. Also in this area are two fine Anglian crosses, known as Acca's cross and the Spital cross, of uncertain attribution.

The floor of the transepts and crossing is paved with slabs, many of which are clearly recycled grave-covers. They came from the many disturbances not only of the Abbey floor, but of the bones buried beneath it. It was until recently thought that the burials within the church had more status than those outside, especially if they could be close to the altar – hardly a Christian view of death. Another disturbance happened when the underfloor heating was inserted in the nineteenth century, which can be traced in the pattern of paving covering the trenches for the heating. Rarely, one can see the whole picture when all the furniture is removed. This can be seen in the etching.

The axis of the Abbey's cross shape is the crossing, with the tower rising above it, supported by pointed arches. The tower is reached from the west along a passage and stairway at the top of the night stair, and houses a fine peal of bells, the latest one added very recently. You will see from the etching that there is no nave to the west, but a blank wall with a pulpit backing onto it, now moved to the sanctuary. It was not until the twentieth century that the nave was added (1907-09), designed by Temple Moore and standing

Above left: Flavinus.

Above right: The east side of the south transept.

on the remains of the south nave wall, still visible. Long before this, when the blocking wall across the west was fitted with a buttress to support the tower, the Saxon crypt came to light. It is not clear whether the whole of the nave was destroyed in raids by Scots or whether in fact it had ever been completed. We move on to the north transept, which to me is one of the most magnificent pieces of architecture in Britain. Again, the east wall is different from the west, for the east has an aisle beyond a line of arches. Although these arches are similarly supported as those in the south transept, they are more elaborate (colour 25, 26).

The west wall has tall lancet windows between semi-octagonal buttresses above a run of arches below that goes all round the transept. The tall lancets at the north are magnificent. Below them, under the running arches, there is new stone. This is where a doorway was added by the Mercers in 1670, which must have threatened the whole structure and was certainly not in keeping with the thirteenth-century design. It was removed in 1740 but fortunately there is still a graphic record of this doorway. Much of the decoration in the transept is original. Notice how some of the sandstone comes from different sources; there is an orange-brown iron-stained coloured sandstone in the north-east which is falling off as sand.

So, before the twentieth-century rebuilding, the Abbey had no nave and appeared as an off-balanced structure. The place where the nave now stands was part of the town graveyard, known as Campy Field. The sanctuary and choir were reached through the Prior Smithson's screen, a rood screen (a rood being a cross) made of wood, with an inscription that commemorates him. 'Mister Thomas Smythson' was prior from 1491-1524, and we are asked to 'pray for his soul'. The screen is very colourful, and the fifteenth-century paintings on it, preserved, are remarkable. They are part of many paintings of the same period that are gems, although many of them have been shuffled around at different times to fit in with

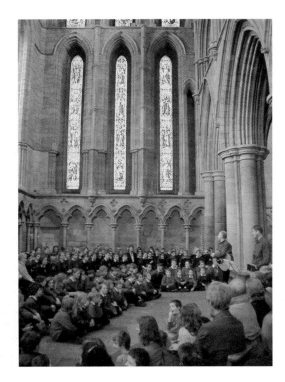

Above left: An etching by T. Allom in 1832 before the nave was added. To the right is the pulpit, since moved to the sanctuary.

Above right: North transept in use.

new tastes (or lack of taste), some only saved later by accident. No one knew, of course, what the early bishops or saints looked like, but that did not prevent the artists from using their imagination. (In the case of the bishops overlooking the sanctuary from the north, their faces are remarkably similar. Wilfrid is depicted not as an Anglian, but dressed in medieval vestments).

At the base of the Smithson screen is a whole row of such figures, but it is possible to know who some of them represent from their names or what they carried. In one, St Cuthbert carries St Oswald's severed head. They are in the same tradition as those in the Etheldreda chapel in the south transept. The new Phelps's organ is supported on this screen, dominating the view from the nave eastward, just as the choir furniture in the crossing dominates that. Perhaps this is a statement about the importance of music in the Abbey.

At the back of the organ is another large screen with paintings of the same period, notably one of a representation of Queen Etheldreda who gave land and income for the church to be built (colour 23). Although it is rather dark at the best of times on these paintings which face the high altar, try to see the one with John and the chalice. The image shows a dragon rising from the chalice as the bare-faced John looks on. There is another with the same story in the Ogle chapel below. John's story is that the devil tempted him to drink from a poisoned chalice. John made the sign of the cross over it, drank its contents, and the devil flew off in the form of a dragon (or 'worm') in frustration. Others depicted on the same projecting 'pulpitum' on the balcony include St Oswald and St Andrew. The figures to the right and left of them on the flat section, five on either side, cannot be easily identified.

The Abbey is full of symbols; the cross itself is the most central, but even here a variation, the saltire cross, depicts the crucifixion of Saint Andrew on a diagonal cross, an image adopted by Prior Leschman

The north transept from the top of the night stair.

on stone as his own. To me the most moving of these old paintings are of Mary, under the arch that leads from nave to chancel. In one, Gabriel announces that Mary is to become the mother of God. The cartouche, or scroll, rather faded, carried the words of what came to be known as 'The Annunciation', the announcement (colour 27). The other picture, opposite, shows Mary meeting Elizabeth, 'The Visitation', to reveal that they are both to have remarkable sons, one Jesus and the other John the Baptist. Trees on a hill in the background point towards the crucifixion, whilst the fortified tower may represent Mary's virginity. Everywhere there are roses ('The Mystic Rose') and lilies, all flowers representing Mary (colour 28).

The imagery in the paintings is at its most graphic in the four panels known as 'The Dance of Death', where the Grim Reaper visits the Pope, Emperor, King and Cardinal to remind them, and us, that we are all equal when we face death, and our earthly status will not save us. These are very rare. Below them is another line of paintings, this time depicting the apostles, identified by their instruments of martyrdom, and some by faded names, arranged on either side of a projecting pulpit which has Christ at the centre. One of the most vivid is that of St Peter, looking very tough, bearded, tonsured, and carrying the keys of Heaven.

Next to these paintings is the entrance to Prior Leschman's chantry, a chantry being a place where prayers were said for the souls of the dead. Many believed that such prayers lessened one's time in Purgatory. Leschman was Prior from 1480-91, and his tomb was covered with a life-sized sculpture of him with a cowl over his eyes. The wooden tracery above him is very finely carved, with additional paintings of St Peter and St Andrew. There is a vivid painting (on a reredos) of Christ rising from his tomb, with all the instruments of the crucifixion around him, with the Prior pictured kneeling before him. Clearly, parts of his tomb have been repositioned, and there are some original pieces of older stone

Top left: Smythson's screen.

Above left: The Phelps's organ, built in 1974 in America.

Above right: John with the chalice, in the Ogle chantry. The detail on the painting has been changed since the fifteenth century.

sculpture included. Outside, by the high altar, are curiously-carved grotesque comic faces in stone; a figure, possibly of St Christopher, stands guard at the tomb.

Opposite, in the early fifteenth-century Ogle chantry, is a 'triptych' (in three parts) with paintings of Mary and baby Jesus on one side and John on the other, with a palm in one hand – a symbol that he was to take care of Mary after Jesus' death, and a dragon rising from the chalice in his left hand. All have a nimbus (halo) that looks as though it was added more recently, and each is surrounded by an elaborate border that speaks of their intense power. Jesus is seen rising from the tomb, painted in a style different from that in the Leschman chantry. The structure was dismantled in 1858, when it was customary to give unwanted material to the people doing the job, and found its way to the Charlton's house at Hesleyside, but was returned to its old place. So much of the Abbey woodwork seen in old etchings has disappeared in this way.

The finest paintings are on the north choir aisle wall. These are nine images of the Passion, full of detail and interest, painted in the fifteenth century. Very vivid in what they portray, the artist has incorporated a medieval Italian background rather than Palestine at the time of Christ. Of particular power and horror is the depiction of the torturers screwing down the crown of thorns on to Jesus' head (colour 24). This stands in complete contrast to the recent icon of Wilfrid in the nearby chapel used for private prayer.

The Dance of Death, one of four panels.

St Peter with the keys to Heaven.

Other survivals of this period are in stone and wood. Opposite the Passion scenes, the wall of the Leschman chantry reveals two periods of sculpture. The lower part, of many subjects flanked at either end by a lion and a kneeling figure with his hands over his ears, is older and in a different tradition from the gallery above it. You might like to try your own interpretation of what the stone figures mean; they have been seen as some of the Deadly Sins. In one, a fox preaching to geese is thought to be a dishonest friar preaching a sermon for his own gain. The one that I find most repellent is the three-faced figure with a diabolical face poking from between its legs and cloven hooves protruding; one of the three heads is a skull and another is a young man's. The rest are symbolic perhaps of theft (the sheep stealer), vanity and gluttony. There is a harpist. The piper is not just a jolly musician, as the bagpipes were regarded as a very coarse instrument. Significantly, Chaucer's lecherous, dishonest Miller led the Pilgrims' procession in *The Canterbury Tales* playing the pipes. In medieval iconography he accompanied the damned to hell.

Above these are some formal leaves, and subjects that include two apostles, Peter and Paul, a version of Celtic interlace, a depiction of St George (or Michael) slaying the dragon and Mary with Jesus' crucified body across her knees, a gluttonous ape and a lily in a vase. There is a row of heads, but not grotesque ones like those on the south side of the tomb. Old drawings show that the tomb was in different parts of the Abbey at different periods of its history.

The Abbey chancel before Dobson's remodelling.

Other sculptures in the aisles are of a different nature. Gilbert de Umfraville (1245-1307) and his wife Elizabeth Comyn may have been buried originally in the lean-to chapel excavated outside the south wall, but the sculpture is now in the south chancel aisle with some pieces missing. A coffin lid in the same aisle, inscribed with shears, the emblem of a woman, belonged to Matilda, wife of a Hexham merchant. The north aisle has a lady's figure from the thirteenth century, quite ghostly in its worn state. There is an effigy of a cross-legged knight, Sir Charles Devilstone, 1297. Elsewhere in the Abbey are some fragments, not easy to arrange, lumped together from many periods, and it would be a good idea to move them one day for display elsewhere. There are so many canons' grave slabs lying around – important to keep, but there is a limit to how many such a building in use for worship can take!

At one time there was a depressing array of military banners commemorating various imperial wars above the people in the nave, but these have now been removed to the north aisle of the nave. It is important to consider what is right to display. The building of the new nave led to considerations like this, and the designers seem to have coped well. However, the display of funeral hatchments along its south wall ought to be reconsidered, especially as these were supposed to be used only once, for the funeral itself; there is always a problem of 'important' people being given prominence, often quite unjustifiably. The Abbey is very well maintained, better than I have known it for over twenty years, but we must not stand still or take things for granted.

Above the altar is a copy of the painting of the Holy Family, the original of which, by Andre del Sarto, (c. 1515), is in the Louvre. Behind it is the Dobson rebuilding of the east end of the Abbey. Finally, the work in wood is nowhere more interesting than the misericords in the choir area of the chancel. 'Misericords' means a plea for the Lord to have mercy, and there is perhaps a gentle irony in that the canons who were able to use the ledges under the seats when they were raised as a rest were grateful at times of prayer when technically they should have been standing upright. The misericords are weird and wonderful creations rather like stone gargoyles that belong to other buildings. It is as though the carpenters have excelled themselves because of the outlet allowed them for their creative imagination. Under the seats there is a triangular piece of wood under the ledge, not seen when the seat is down, that

The stone screen.

was, in many cases throughout Britain, highly decorated, with creatures like the Green Man, probably a pagan fertility symbol, depicted with tendrils coming from his mouth to form leaves round his head. In stone, there is a parallel in the table tomb between the north choir aisle and the north transept, where a male and female head each spout growths which form into vine leaves, the vine representing the blood of Christ and eternal life. Thus, 'I am the vine, and you are the branches'. Not all the symbolism of the misericords is clear. There are beasts with pronounced teeth, and angels with bats' wings. With the flowers, the roses refer usually to Mary. There are shields. Some have been added in recent times to make up for missing ones.

It is not only the seats that have this elaborate carving; two arm rests have that powerful image of the pelican feeding her babies with her blood, the belief being that she was saving their lives, as Christ saved ours. It was meant to be a sacrifice (in fact the pelican smears oil from her own feathers to lubricate her babies' feathers). It is a tender and significant image, present in other churches, (on the lectern in Warkworth, for example). In Shakespeare's *King Lear*, the King speaks of his 'pelican daughters' who were draining away his power.

The remarkable survival of so many important paintings and wood and stone sculptures is made more interesting (and distressing) by the way in which these things have been moved around the Abbey. Many objects have been brought in from outside, like Acca's cross, and there is one object exhibited in the south choir aisle that shows just how great the upheavals were; the chalice, late Saxon or early Norman, was found in 1860 in a coffin when a trench was dug for heating-pipes. It is so small that it was probably intended to be used with a portable altar to take the sacrament outside before it was eventually buried in a funeral service. It is touching to think of it doing the rounds, bringing comfort and support to local people. Another object is the beautifully carved Jacobean cover over the font, the latter probably recycled from Roman stone. Over all is an even more elaborate canopy, carved in 1916 by a Flemish refugee, incorporating fifteenth-century wood. So far from home, he must have found solace in this act of creation, rather like those Italian prisoners of war on Orkney who built their church out of any materials that came to hand.

There is much more that I have not mentioned, such as a whole array of stained-glass windows belonging to recent times, but you, the visitor, will find in the Abbey a great deal of information that will help you with your interests.

The Abbey is anything but a museum, and it attracts a variety of displays and contemporary works of art. In January, for example, it hosted the Golden Tapestry exhibition, filling the building with marvellous colour, the work of school children from the Commonwealth (colour 22). A recent tapestry, hanging on the south wall of the nave, is the Hexham Millennium Banner, made by local embroiderers to celebrate the town and its history.

The latest piece of sculpture to be displayed in limestone is the Tsunami Noni. Sculpted by Rosie Musgrave, it is a lovely figure of a woman lying in a boat awaiting transformation. Named by Sri Lankans who were caught up in the devastation, it is dedicated to those who were drowned. Its presence on the flagstones of the north transept, especially with sunlight pouring through the windows, is a reminder that no man or woman is an island, but that we are all part of common humanity, sharing everything. This book will now follow other themes in the history of Hexham, particularly when they relate to what is still visible.

STREETS

The streets that converge on the Market Place are intrinsically interesting, and to look carefully at the buildings in them tells us yet more about the history of the town. The Shambles backs onto a line of shops that covers the medieval church of St Mary, under which an even older church might lie.

St Mary's Chare

As you go through a small arch into St Mary's Chare (or Back Street, as it is also known), you enter a narrow road that looks medieval, with buildings on either side. Turn round and look at the wall of the buildings pierced by this arch where there are pointed arches, one springing from its pillar in a wall that is part stone and part brick. The photograph included later in this chapter shows how altered it is.

The blocked arch has been partly unblocked in the deep past and a window inserted, then this too was blocked. At once this is recognised as church architecture, with quite different uses over time. The panel in the Market Place has faithfully established what the church might have looked like before it was almost completely swallowed up by later building. In the cellar of a watch maker's shop by the arch is the undercroft of the church, with the arch-supports visible, and in Paxton's fish and chip shop (a 'Plaice in History' as Peter Ryder calls it) there are the remains of a bread oven displayed that once took advantage of a redundant building, as other shops and houses did. As we have seen, the church had long gone out of service before the Priory was dissolved, giving a reason for the Priory church to be retained as a town church without the canons. The red brick above the arch has 'church-type' windows facing north and south, and inside the flats on the staircase is a very fine medieval arch, covered with wallpaper when I first saw it.

Older photographs were kept as a record of another part of the arched nave, now replaced by Dickinson's furnishings, and much more recently, during extensions to the same premises, small fragments of the old church were also found. A spate of fires caused some recent rebuilding and an opportunity to examine structures archaeologically, confirming what we know about this building. There are some old drawings and photographs that enable us to piece together the history of the Chare, with

Children with the Tsunami Noni.

sufficient structure left in places to locate them. A row of buildings going off to the east to join Fore Street is collectively known as Meal Market, with the oldest recorded building there, now destroyed, dating from the seventeenth century. There are drawings of it; in 1883 its decorated doorway was removed by William Heron to West End Terrace, at the other end of town, another one of Hexham's wandering doorways. The Meal Market is now occupied by a newsagent's, butcher, offices, and one side of a café. When the road was being cobbled recently, part of it collapsed as it was built over a cellar which was once a store for Robinson's, now Boots', where we recorded an arch of stone and brick.

This is a reminder that there were many cellars throughout Hexham, under the pavements and roads and under existing buildings, for as there was pressure on the town centre for more storage and living space, it paid to dig deeper. This also gave rise to rumours that tunnels were connected to the Abbey, though we are not told why.

The north buildings of St Mary's Chare back onto the Priory wall, the oldest part of this still standing behind The George and Dragon Inn, now a finely restored seventeenth-century courtyard building, with its surviving seventeenth-century windows, attics and part of its frontage added to by fine replicas. A well came to light within the courtyard during clearance, but was refilled and covered over.

The rebuilding includes a tasteful reinstatement of one of the few surviving parts of the Priory wall. The site had been used for various other purposes since its closure as an inn in 1937, including a dance studio, and the handling of the new building has been expert in plan and execution; indeed, it is one of Hexham's finest achievements.

Within the same street is The Grapes Inn, an 1899 brick-and-stone building that covers a demolished sixteenth-century inn. Again, old illustrations enable us to know what it looked like as it is pictured from front and rear. Of similar quality to the Old Tannery at Cockshaw, this inn has stained-glass windows and ceramic tiles. Built into the front, a survival of something older, are the arms of Thomas Lord Dacre, the bailiff of Hexhamshire from 1514-32. The brick building which links it to the arch has undergone many changes; the house in which the famous Dr Joseph Parker, president of the Free Church Council, was born in 1830 was part of it until it was demolished in 1904.

Other buildings on the Chare vary in age, height and attractiveness. Offset from the line of the other buildings, once one of Hexham's many places of worship, is the 1862 Primitive Methodist Hebbron Chapel, now a beauty salon. The opposite side of the Chare, backing onto Fore Street, has been taken

St Mary's church arches, built
into a wall.

A medieval arch of the church
found during demolition work
at the back of Dickinson's
furnishings in 1904.

General view of
St Mary's Chare.

over by modern shops such as Boots' and Woolworth's. The former has preserved a bow-fronted shop window, and the latter has yet another recycled seventeenth-century doorway built into it, previously on the other side of the road!

What is striking about the arrangement of buildings in the Chare is that there are still echoes of the strips of land, often referred to as 'burgages', which contained a house, garden or yard often packed with pig sties and working areas, to say nothing of their function as repositories for rubbish, including night soil. We know the names of many of the owners of these strips from as long ago as the seventeenth century from documents (only recently unearthed and studied by Anna Rossiter). The northern ones backed on to the Priory wall and after the Dissolution accessed the Abbey Grounds by doorways. The building of Beaumont Street presumably stopped any further unofficial access. It is worth inspecting the area between the wall and the road, for here we see a mixture of old and new brick and stone characteristic of Hexham in general. The buildings are aligned on the old strip pattern, roughly at right angles to the wall. There is a fine Venetian window incorporated in one, and parts of the Priory wall include blocked doorways.

On the opposite side of the Chare are the strips that existed right through to Fore Street. The same system was in use to the north of the Market Place until the redevelopment of the site of Pudding Mews, which missed a great opportunity to examine the pattern archaeologically in sufficient detail before rebuilding took place. The Chare now has the backs of large shops, although there are still some premises that are interesting, such as an Italian restaurant above a shop, where the stonework has been restored to fit the character of the place.

Among the recently established shops is that of 'Cogito', its name derived from that famous dictum proving man's existence, used by Descartes: *'Cogito Ergo Sum'*– I think and therefore I am. 'Ergo' has been adopted by the publishing side of the shop's business, a welcome addition to local publishing of Northern material.

The George and Dragon Inn courtyard during restoration.

The courtyard today. The building dates from 1663-85.

A general view behind the Priory wall. These buildings probably pre-date 1700.

A brick late eighteenth-century building with a fine Venetian window has been built on the line of the Priory wall (right).

Beaumont Street and the Abbey Grounds

North of St Mary's Chare and roughly parallel to it is Beaumont Street, named after the landowner, the Lord of the Manor, and created in a short time to provide a new road out of the Market Place. Built at his expense, it cut through the former Priory grounds.

This has some very fine Victorian buildings made from sandstone backing on to the Priory wall to the south. The Queen's Hall takes pride of place, now the town library, theatre, café, meeting rooms, art galleries and a centre of culture. Looking very French in many ways, it faces the Abbey Grounds, parkland that is accessed by an arch that used to be part of the White Hart Hotel yard in Fore Street, closed in 1916 and demolished in 1929. Mr Robb gave the arch as a war memorial to the Northumberland Fusiliers, and it joins one of many arches that have been repositioned in the town.

The Queen's Hall originated in 1857 when the Corn Exchange Company was formed to control agricultural trade and needed a building for weekly markets. It opened in 1866 with the Corn Exchange at the centre, the town hall and local Board of Health in one wing and Lambton's bank in the other (colour 9). The town hall was taken over by the Hexham Entertainment Company in 1920 and used as a cinema which became known as the Queen's Hall. It closed in 1976, was bought by the District and County Council and opened as an arts centre in 1983. The building next to it, separated by St Mary's Wynd (a small lane), was owned by Temperley and Co., a name that appears on other buildings in the town. It is well built in sandstone, of similar quality to the Queen's Hall, and is now largely flats to the rear, with a dentist's and shops in front. The small car park at the back separates it from the old Priory wall.

The panel at the top of Beaumont Street shows the changes that have taken place since the building of Trinity Methodist church. Not only is this building used for services, but also for many activities that demand space, such as children's activities, meetings and talks, for which it has excellent facilities. Next to it is the Beaumont Hotel, currently on the market for £2 million. The hotel, first named the Abbey Hotel in 1902, was a Temperance Hotel, but changed its name when it became licensed in 1953. The site of both the Central Methodist church (completed in 1909) and the hotel was once an auction mart.

The Queen's Hall behind the morris dancers.

A popular postcard issued to show the attractions of the Queen's Hall. The ballroom is now the library.

The changes seen in old photographs include the apparent traffic-free access, although photographers such as the locally famous Gibsons could control the scene so that there was no movement to blur the picture. There was a wall on the park side of the road, later removed, now replaced by iron railings, and the trees have now matured.

The rest of the street houses *The Hexham Courant*'s offices, flats above shops, and other buildings opposite the Abbey. The upheavals resulting from the building of this road affected part of the Priory and its graveyard and the Abbey Grounds; photographs record some of this, with gaping holes where trees have been uprooted.

An arch gives access to the Abbey Grounds, and further up the street is a set of gates and railings donated by the Benson family to the town when the grounds were opened as a public park in 1911. Recently the grounds have been restored to their Victorian pattern, very successfully. Paths focus on the bandstand, donated by Henry Bell (the fellmonger), a centre for many lively concerts and events (colour 11, 12, 13). The line of the old Priory wall, not the original stonework, still encloses the parkland, separating it from the higher open space called the Sele, surrounded largely by lime trees. Although

The information panel at the top of Beaumont Street. (Courtesy of Hexham Historic Partnership)

the Sele has had paths across it in the past and recreational buildings, it is now an open space looking north to the River Tyne and the north ridge of the valley. An often-overlooked feature of the Sele grounds is a cast-iron drinking fountain erected in 1899 by the Abbey Church of England Temperance Society as a memorial to Queen Victoria's Silver Jubilee (colour 19). Like so many others of its kind, it has a heron as its centrepiece, symbolising pure water, and an inscription, 'Keep the pavements dry'. I have taken many evocative photographs at all seasons through this piece of ironwork, looking out to the slope of the Sele bank and its trees. Behind it, the Sele First School, conveniently sited near to a good playground and sports field, has had two phases of building, in 1856 and 1915.

Taken all together, this extensive parkland is an enormous asset to the town and has resisted any development except to the enhancement of its beauty. Its most northerly enclosure by the old Priory wall, where it meets Market Street and Gilesgate, includes the Halgut Burn and its willows and other lovely trees, leading to Hexham House, overlooking a bowling green. It was built in 1723 by the Reverend Thomas Andrewes. The wings were added in the nineteenth century. His title was 'rector and Lecturer of the Abbey'; the term 'Lecturer' came about when people with specific oratorical skills were appointed to give sermons, as these might not have been successfully handled by a parish priest.

After the prior was dismissed at the Dissolution, the grounds became a large garden for the new owners. This is why they survived any encroachment from the town, even though space for building was at a premium. Hexham House was an exception. Its garden was later turned into what we now see as the bowling green, but before this the house and land belonged to Hexham House School (1915-1926) after which it was sold to be used as a public library (colour 17). It was eventually taken over as council offices, which it still is, with the Green Flag Award flying above it. The old Priory gateway marks the limit of its territory, with the long bowling green clubhouse lining the road to the house of Carnaby, the first domestic building to be constructed out of the Priory. Before that, part of it had been for the use of the priors themselves, with a significant building still carrying the emblems of Prior Leschman. The garden is connected to the Cloisters by an arch, and from here one is back in Beaumont Street.

The Hexham Courant offices.

The Memorial Arch, *c.* 1685.

View through the drinking fountain to the Sele.

Hexham House and bowling green.

The landscape of the Abbey Grounds continues to be improved. There is now next to Hexham House a 'Sensory Garden', a little haven of rest, originally designed for blind people, open to all, behind which the Halgut Burn continues its way to the old tannery sites. The grounds are an asset too on bonfire night, using the height advantage of the Sele, and for the fireworks display, seen by thousands of people. It is also a place for sledges, a place to practise skateboard techniques, a safe playground for children, and a place to stroll or to listen to music or to share in one of the many festivals held there. The western boundary is the Cockshaw Burn, now landscaped into an accessible area with a stream and woodland.

The Benson statue, erected in 1904 by public subscription, commemorates Colonel Benson, killed in the Boer War by a sniper (as the story has it, the binoculars he carried reflected the sun and made him a target). It represents the admiration in which he, his family, and fellow soldiers were held, but it is also a reminder that the British were responsible for the concentration camps in which thousands of Boer women and children died. Life is so often double-faced.

Hencotes, Battle Hill and Priestpopple

The dark statue faces the road that runs through Hexham from east to west into which Fore Street, St Mary's Chare and Eastgate now run. To the west it goes to Hencotes, where there are some stone and brick buildings away from the town centre, some backing onto the Sele wall with attractive hidden gardens.

Yet another church was founded here, a Congregational church built in 1869 and demolished in 1967, on a site where new houses face St Cuthbert's Terrace. Hencotes also has shops of many kinds, all within easy reach of the town centre, and some very elegant houses, including Georgian, Regency and Victorian buildings.

Closer to the statue are two churches that are still being used: St Mary's church and the United Reformed church, with its established date clearly visible, 1824. To the east, the road is called Battle Hill, probably named after the Old English for a hill with a building. Yet another church, still existing as the Hexham Community church, stands with its castle-like round towers on the corner. Opposite is a fine stone-built Victorian house, reflecting the confidence of its period.

The Sensory Garden.

Sledging on the Sele, looking north towards the Tyne valley.

A Boer War hero, Colonel Benson.

Part of Hencotes.

To the east are the remains, just an arch, of the birthplace of Wilfrid Wilson Gibson, a poet, son of John Gibson. Changes in Hexham have been rapid, so attempts to put names to premises in a book like this are futile in many cases. Charity shops benefit from closures of other businesses, and not only fill vacant premises but are popular and successful: three out of seven are found in Battle Hill alone, all selling good-quality recycled items.

Further down this road was the United Presbyterian church, built in 1863 and demolished in 1954 to make way for a post office, in its turn recently demolished to make way for a red-brick block of flats (Stainthorpe Court) that join buildings of artificial stone fronts. These merge into the large 'Excelsior' building, a late nineteenth-century red-brick block with an arched entrance.

One interesting feature on the north side is part of the old Priory wall built into a dentist's, marking its course past the Benson statue to the United Reformed church, where it turned to run north. At this point are two interesting buildings, both group surgeries now. It is difficult to imagine that in the early twentieth century, cattle were still walked to market down this road. On the north side, where St Mary's Chare joined the road, there are the buildings of yet another redundant inn, 'The Grey Bull', which had the name 'Thomas Oliver and Sons' painted above it. It closed in 1990 and became flats above shops.

The road is joined by Eastgate, or the Skinners' Burn, at the opposite end of Fore Street. This junction used to be the Cattle Market. On the corner of Eastgate is the 'Tap and Spile', with a Gothic-type window above it, occupying the former site of a post office and the 'Criterion Hotel'. Underneath the road junction, there was a recent opportunity to look at a forgotten piece of Hexham's history: the culverted Skinners' Burn, accessed by manhole covers when the road was up, for underneath are tunnels of brick and stone recorded by Peter Ryder, who crawled through them with compass, tape and notebook until it became too wet! My duty, from a distance, was to ensure that he did not disappear.

The complexity of changing ownership and use of premises is no better seen than in the history of the banks, which are all concentrated here and the road's extension, called Priestpopple (which originally meant small plots of land occupied or owned by priests). The fine building at the end of Fore Street, rounded, with its evocative frieze, belongs to HSBC, but in 1896 it was built for the Carlisle City and District Bank, became the London City and District Bank, and took its present name in 1999. It is built of red sandstone, with decoration that includes sovereigns, shillings and pence, small naked figures and foliage. The banks have some of the most modern classic-style architecture in town.

The top of Battle Hill.

Battle Hill, with the arch of Gibson's
house and new building.

Excelsior Building.

The Criterion Hotel, now the Tap and Spile, at the Old Cattle Market, to which cattle are being driven.

An old picture of Battle Hill into Priestpopple.

The Barclays Bank building was a bank in 1899, and changed owners several times, including being used by Lloyds. It has an Arts-and-Crafts frieze. Above the entrance to the present Lloyds Bank is a stone carving which shows that it belonged to Lambton and Co., one of the first banks to trade in the town in 1895. Lloyds took over in 1908. It is built of brick and rusticated blocks of grey granite.

Across the road was another bank, TSB, incorporated now with Lloyds. The building is currently used as a betting shop. The other existing bank is the National Westminster, at the end of St Mary's Chare, made of smooth sandstone blocks above granite which curve around the corner.

On the same side of the road, further east is the Royal Hotel with its distinctive gold-painted dome, with the County Hotel on the other side of the road, just below an elegantly functional stone-built County Mills, now converted to offices and accommodation.

Where the roundabout halts traffic momentarily there are early nineteenth-century stone houses with Greek-style porticoes, called Orchard House and Orchard Place, where the road turns north to

The HSBC bank.

Lloyds bank.

the railway station. It was when underpinning was taking place at the latter, at the Wentworth turning, that an old private well was exposed, one of many marked on old maps. We have recorded and photographed this stone-lined shaft.

The new hospital, replacing a series of rectangular huts, now dominates the roundabout, leading on to the Corbridge road eastward, with the old Workhouse to the left (this will be described later). Opposite the hospital, along Priestpopple once again, is a recently-built curved building that gets away from the solid squareness and squat buildings in the vicinity.

The Wentworth car park, where an attendant pretends to 'book' a veteran Ford car during a large rally.

The way back to Market Street

You can return to the Market Place via Loosing Hill, past the Railway Inn (formerly the North British), a red-brick building, following the Wentworth car park and the leisure centre along a wide path that gives a view of sheltered housing on one side and the expanse of new shops and industry to the north. Here is the Information Centre and the main council car park. The Leisure Centre, about to be expanded with the addition of a 25-metre, 6-lane pool, is a great asset. There is a steep climb up to the Old Gaol which emphasises the fact that Hexham is built high above the river and its banks. To the right are gardens belonging to Prospect House, and to the left some old brick buildings that give way to stone. Here we are at the back of the Fore Street shops. A narrow lane leading into Fore Street is often a source of complaint, but it does show the arrangement of strips of land mentioned elsewhere in this chapter. For those who have struggled to climb the hill from the car park, there is aesthetic and other refreshment at The Gallery Café opposite the Old Grammar School. There is a small cobbled space behind Argos known as the Goose Market. A café, the intriguingly-named Phat Katz, nestles below the gaol, and The Athena is positioned on the corner by the Moothall, which we now pass to re-enter Market Place.

Market Street and Gilesgate

Old pictures and surviving buildings show that some of the finest seventeenth-century houses were built in Market Street, which changes its name to Gilesgate beyond the arch that leads to the Abbey. One particularly fine house, at the entrance to the market, had been demolished by 1900 (see Kristenson and Dallison, 2006, for a picture). One building that has survived is now a hairdresser's, Nos 20 and 22, an elegant, well-balanced structure flanked by two bays, its centre having two doors with scrolled decoration over them similar to that on the Old Grammar School and The George and Dragon Inn, technically know as bolection-moulded doorways with curly open segmental pediments (Pevsner, 330).

Further north were similar buildings, in a state of last-gasp ruination, photographed by J.P. Gibson, who was awarded a diploma for it by the Photographic Society of Philadelphia. These were demolished in 1885, when Henry Bell, the fellmonger, built a wool warehouse on the site. It is now a swimming

A seventeenth-century town house (c. 1685) in Market Street.

pool, a splendid example of retaining part of an old building to incorporate into a new one; it won a European Architectural Heritage Award (colour 18). This in turn is scheduled to change in function again when the new swimming pool is built at the Wentworth Centre. Next to it is the Community Centre. The other great building of the seventeenth century, Holy Island House, is featured later in this book in chapter three.

Market Street, via Gilesgate, was a principal route in and out of Hexham, and continued to attract buildings of quality. Opposite the Priory gate is the former post office, now Hadrian House, three storeys high and built in five bays in the mid-eighteenth century. Further south are shop fronts with mullion type windows and deep cellars, with more recent building in the shape of the Salvation Army citadel and 'The Heart of all England' inn.

Haugh Lane and Hallstile Bank

Haugh Lane, named after the flat alluvial land that flanks the river, lies at the north end of Market Street and Gilesgate, leading out of town via Eilansgate (or Helensgate) and Quatre Bras towards the A69.

Its continuation eastward is a messy collection of small buildings and crammed unofficial parking that does not benefit by having so many garages of different sizes along its path. This has replaced a landscape of market gardens, also covered with many kinds of industries and offices. At a major roundabout one branch of the road goes into the large Tesco complex, and the other leads uphill to the Market Place again, by way of Hallstile Bank, but before taking this road on foot, notice the site of one of the two roperies in Hexham at Orchard Terrace. These were long thin buildings originally; only one is now visible, near to the Co-op car park on the south side of the town, dilapidated, and it is difficult to find a new use for it because of its unusual long rectangular shape and low roof.

At the bottom of Hallstile Bank is an attractive row of the Henry King Memorial Almshouses, built in Tudor style in 1891, with another one of Hexham's wandering archways of around 1700 leading into it. The cellar visible at the top end of the street may be on the site of a tower on the wall that possibly surrounded the civil administrative centre, but there are interesting buildings on either side of this road too. On the right-hand side is a row of stone houses built in 1888 by Thomas Ellis on a ruined site. Opposite

Alms Houses, 1893, with a seventeenth-century gateway.

The former Primitive Methodist Chapel of 1830, converted into houses.

there is a house that makes one pause, as its large gable end has two doors side by side below it. The house had a plaque, now illegible, to say that it was in 1830 a Primitive Methodist Chapel. This closed in 1863 and converted into two houses.

Below it, fine stonework has been refaced. Above the chapel some Georgian houses were demolished in 1967 (pictured in Kristensen and Dallison on page 30). The sad story continues further up the hill, where more Georgian houses had already been demolished in 1890 (ibid). The remains of these houses included steps which had replaced a shop, and then we are into the remains of the late seventeenth-century vaulted cellar below Prospect House. Opposite, leading further up to the Market Place, are some fine stone-fronted houses at a high level above the road, recently given a facelift. Behind them, the land begins to fall away to the valley, and on the slope are remnants of other buildings, now unused. At the top of the bank is an island of buildings facing the Market Place, behind which is The Forum Cinema, once called The Gem Picture Palace. Joining it on one side is Wetherspoon's and on the other, Pudding Mews, built over a medieval site. A little lane, Back Row, links these to Market Street.

The Gibson shop in Fore Street.

Fore Street (Coastley Row)

Fore Street, or Coastley Row as it used to be called, is now regarded as the principal shopping street. Attractively pedestrianised, it has a variety of buildings of all shapes, sizes and styles that reflect changing tastes, not all good ones. Unfortunately, according to the modern practice, a travesty of good window-dressing, the windows are plastered with garish advertisements, none more so than the shop at present occupying what used to be Gibson and Sons' chemists and opticians. John Gibson was one of the most important citizens of Hexham, and the ornate frontage of his shop was designed when his son became a Freeman of the Worshipful Company of Spectacle Makers. His grandson was also to become a Freeman. What is so interesting about the designed shop front is that its carvings were made by one of the many Belgian refugees in Hexham during the First World War, Josephus Ceulemans, to thank the Gibsons for their generosity to them. The frontage was copied by the Science Museum in London and all its fittings transferred there.

I have mentioned only one shop, to show how ownership and function change. As you walk along the street you can read many of these changes, and there are booklets that display pictures of the premises as they were. It is difficult to think of this road being open to traffic at all times, yet it is only recently that it has been pedestrianised.

The Pattinsons were an interesting and successful family, not only in England, but abroad. Helen Baker has researched pharmacist Pattinsons in Australia and Canada, for example in *The Hexham Historian* Volume 16 (2006). In Australia, Lewy Pattinson named his house in the heart of Sidney on a 26-acre estate 'Hexham'. It was built on the success of his chemist's shop, warehouse and laboratories. By 1890, he and his brother had opened five shops and a head office, taken on a partner, and by the turn of the century had a warehouse, factory and sixteen shops, including a factory for making their own medicine bottles. To show how successful they were, in 1940 Lewy was able to donate the first aeroplane to the Royal Flying Doctor Service. He died at the age of ninety-two. Today in Hexham the name Pattinson is still evident in a pharmacy and photographer's at the end of Fore Street.

Old photographs show inns that have disappeared, especially 'The White Hart Hotel', where magistrates once held petty sessions for Tynedale. Further north was 'The Sun Inn'. After The White Hart

Fore Street.

The north end of Fore Street; some changes have taken place in the short time since this picture was taken.

was closed in 1916, its arch was given as a war memorial opposite the Queen's Hall and the inn was demolished in 1929. Whenever changes are made to turn premises into modern shops, there is the reminder that underlying all buildings is an ancient plan of strips of land that used to be the norm for town properties. One of the oldest to survive was William Robb's, who built new shops there in 1890, 1901, and 1960, and whose name still stands.

Where the street enters the Market Place, on the west side, used to be the east end of the medieval chapel that once served the people of Hexham before it became abandoned as such and given over to houses, bakeries and shops.

Many of the shops have a major common fault in that very little notice has been taken of their setting when it comes to designing a shop front. The universal logos of these shops can be very ugly and inappropriate to an attractive small town. This account has outlined the interest to be found in an exploration of Hexham's central streets. This is what we see today. Now I shall return to a deeper past to trace more developments in Hexham's history.

Chapter 2

Living on the Edge: Violence and Survival

The fact that the Old Gaol has been converted into a centre for the study of the Border reminds us that the history of a Border town is going to be different from others further south, although all places have experienced war and lawlessness. What makes this Border different is that it involves not only tension and warfare between England and Scotland, where it played a part in the ambitions and policies of kings, but among the Border people themselves. Here local tribal ambitions under the various 'surnames' – such as Armstrong and Hall – produced what amounted to a mafia. There was nothing romantic about this, despite some people's attempts to put a gloss on \ was often bloody and very cruel, sometimes a fight for survival, and sometimes a working out of individual ambition. The Borderers were not simply Scots or English; many had land and kinship links in both countries, and the Border was a place where loyalties could frequently change from one side to another. At the Battle of Flodden in the north of the county in 1513, the fiercest and bloodiest of all battles between Scots and English, people from the Border could be found fighting on either side, or taking advantage of the conflict to take from both.

The Chronicle of Lanercost (1272-1346) tells of the Scots' invasion of the northern areas, which included Hexham, in which they 'surpassed in cruelty all the fury of the heathen', holding aloft little children on spikes, locking children in a school and burning them to death, raping and killing indiscriminately – even though the church was dedicated to their patron saint, they destroyed it. The chronicler was obviously drawing on events that actually might have happened, and squeezed the last drop of horror out of it. Nothing was sacred, and these madmen 'reached such a pitch of iniquity as to fling contemptuously into the flames the relics of the saints preserved in shrines, tearing off them the gold and silver plates and gems. Also, roaring with laughter, they cut the head off the image of St Andrew, a conspicuous figure, declaring he must leave that place and return to his own soil to be trodden under foot.' (Maxwell, 1913).

Wallace, after his victory at Stirling Bridge, raided the north in the following year, making the Priory his headquarters, and pledged that no harm should come to the people or their lands. Whether this was honoured or not by his troops was another matter. Some people have attributed molten lead on the night stair to this period, suggesting that the nave (rebuilt in the early twentieth century) was destroyed at this time, but this is not certain. However, things were so bad after this that the *Inspeximus* of the following year had to be carried out because all the Priory's documents had been destroyed, and Edward I ordered 'the honest, lawful men' to testify upon oath what 'the Prior and convent' legally held in and around the town and church. It is, of course, a useful document in that it describes the extent of their holdings. Other documents at later dates (especially 1232 and 1328) add to these. Hexham was granted a Market Place extension in 1350, but as the market declined, in 1385 the Lord of Coastley (west of the town) allowed the southern part of it to be developed for housing. Fore Street used to be known as Coastley Row.

I have tried to envisage what it meant to people living on the Borders when such raids happened, and I have chosen to write this as a poem:

The Scots

They poured along the valleys from the north
Like molten pitch, burning, destroying all before their way.
The Scots rampaged, a bloodlust veiled their eyes,
And they forgot the child they murdered could have been their own.
And they forgot despair of crops destroyed,
Of butchered kyle and slaughtered sheep,
For what they did was in a different world.
Damnation for their deeds returned in sleep.
For they would see the Priory burn,
The desecration of the cherished bones,
The beauty of creation broken down,
Destruction of the House of God,
Destruction of the people's town.

At their retreat they left a broken dream
And real lives lost to butchery and greed
A smoking heap of ruins laced with human bones.
Blood will have blood;
The English were to do the same
And back and forward armies marched
As people on the Borders caught the blast
Of hatred and of politics gone mad.

The nave became a graveyard for the town,
Bones piled on bones, covering Saint Wilfrid's crypt.
It waited centuries, for a more enlightened, peaceful age
To clear away the horror and renew the nave.
We are but dust, and must to dust return,
But we are the fire of inspiration that will burn
To recreate the town of Hexham and the House of God.

The facts tell us that, although trade declined and there were horrendous episodes from attacks, as Hexham was in the front line, life had to go on. It is inconceivable that the Border was always at war, as one cannot imagine anyone surviving a period that extended for about 300 years. Rather like the history of the Roman wall, we have to remember that there were long periods of peace, and that some people never experienced a battle or attack. Conditions were supposed to have improved when the Scottish king, James VI, united the crowns when he became James I of England in 1603, and that is

307 years after the first attack described above. The dramatic events tend to be those reported: as with some modern newspapers, the ordinary does not attract attention. Both English and Scottish soldiers undoubtedly committed atrocities, and local people would have 'supped full of horrors' when they came. The Border was undoubtedly troubled, as English and Scottish governments kept it as a buffer state between them where different rules applied.

Another point to remember is that the Border is not all the same. The east has large areas of fertile arable land in the valleys and on the coastal plain. Most of the higher ground would support many sheep and cattle, and it was here where rustling mainly took place, where the food was 'on the hoof', there were plenty of places to hide stolen herds, and locals knew the difficult terrain better than some of their pursuers. It was not in the interests of those farming the rich arable lands to be in a perpetual state of warfare, and many of the local Border lords saw that it was in their interest not to be at each other's throats all the time. The land was covered with defences ranging from full-blown castles like Alnwick and Warkworth and Berwick to the hundreds of smaller fortified towers that provided a base for lesser leaders. As times became more peaceful, these towers and castles began to show signs of change in their design; more light, more luxury, a breakaway from the grim fortress.

The Priory had been attacked and sacked in the late thirteenth century, and Tynedale people were as guilty of raids and violations as anywhere else along the Border, so it is no wonder that this acted as a great check on any expansion and prosperity of Hexham. Some of the 'atmosphere' of this borderland is captured in the unique traditional ballads, the genuine ones being a curious mixture of reality and the supernatural, and some were records of battles and skirmishes, such as Chevy Chase and the Battle of Otterburn, demonstrating the kinds of conflict that lords dragged people into. People needed protection; towns offered that to some extent, but you might attach yourself to a powerful small chieftain, taking his name as your own, and offering to fight for him in return for his protection. This loyalty went across boundaries, and you might be a Scot or Englishman fighting against your own nationals. If someone sacked your home, burnt your crops and drove off your herds, you sought a way to get your own back by allegiance to a strong leader. It was rather like the Scottish clan system. It was never a simple system of knowing who your enemy was, for people changed sides according to self-advantage. Being English or Scottish was not the crucial thing.

Within this spread of towns, villages, fields and upland pastures with their tempting pickings, there was some kind of rule of law. It was not all anarchy. There were Wardens of the Marches (defined areas) who were responsible to their sovereigns for maintaining law and order, and although there was inevitable corruption through self-interest and personal loyalties, the system worked to some extent. Love and attraction could override the borders, some men preferring the women in another surname group, and vice versa.

A collection of Border papers over many years tells many of these stories and shows us how the rule of law worked, or didn't. If you are in Hexham for any length of time, you may wish to read some there, where they are easily accessible. Some are in the Old Gaol, itself built during this turbulent time. They contain much information, many stories and songs, but great gaps in our knowledge still remain of what has come to be called the Reiver Period (the word meaning that you were bereft of your goods by them; they were thieves). Meanwhile the Priory did go on being modified and added to in this period, as we can see. The canons were under the protection of the Lord of the Manor, who was also the Archbishop of York, but if the worst came to the worst there was not much that could be done against sudden raids, except perhaps to retreat behind strengthened walls.

One episode in the town's history in the period before the Union of the Crowns was known as the Battle of Hexham. Really it was a small-scale affair, a skirmish rather than a battle, but it captured

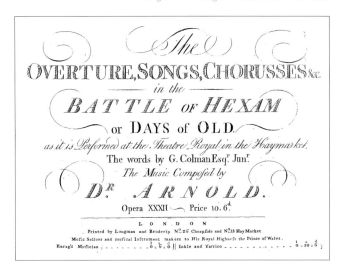

The Battle of Hexham: original cover of
the music.

the imagination long after. It took place in 1464, part of the Wars of the Roses. The Yorkists had been triumphant, but Northumberland generally remained pro-Lancastrian. Henry, Duke of Somerset, made his last stand for the Lancastrians at a site near Hexham, but still not a certain one. He was defeated by Lord Montague, and had his head cut off along with the other 'rebels'. He was supposedly buried in the Abbey.

The rest of England remembered it as a musical made of a story that the queen, with her son, had wandered into a wood at the time the battle was lost and had thrown herself on the mercy of an outlaw. He at once gave her his aid and arranged their escape. In the Local History Society we not only recovered this entire story, but the music too, and performed some of it at an Annual General Meeting of the Society with the help of members and the Abbey Choir. As we regarded this as a major discovery, I shall give a little more detail.

The Battle of Hexham

The society has a membership of over 200, and is very active, especially in research. The script was discovered through the Hexham History Society newsletter. It was written by George Coleman the younger, who belonged to the family that owned the Haymarket Theatre in the late eighteenth century in London, and the play opened a month after the fall of the Bastille in 1789. It was also performed in Hartlepool in 1854. It is based on the mythical encounter between Gondibert, a robber in the Forest of Hexham, and Queen Margaret. This could not have happened as she was out of the country at the time. Adeline, a young woman, leaves her children to follow her runaway husband, Gondibert, whose loyalty to the Lancastrians has brought trouble to himself and his family – he beat up some Yorkists. Adeline dresses as a man (shades of Shakespeare) and takes with her an old retainer, Gregory Gubbins, on her journey to the camp at Hexham, where she expects to find her husband. Gregory finds the going tough. We are introduced to the comic element: a drummer, fifer, corporal and soldiers of the Lancastrian camp, then another stock character, the fool, the jester with his ready wit and supposed insight into human affairs. He meets Adeline and Gregory. Enter Queen Margaret, speaking blank verse instead of prose, bemoaning the lack of respect from all except her flatterer, Le Varenne of Normandy. All the men

The outlaw confronting the queen: engraving from the 1808 edition of
The Battle of Hexham (Inchbald).

are itching for a fight. The queen and Adeline exchange words and we are introduced to the young
Prince of Wales, a dutiful son who regrets that he is not big enough to fight for his mother's sake. The
queen is courageous (although Gregory observes her as 'the lady with the brass basin on her head').

The battle is quickly over, the fool finds out who has won and declares his loyalty to the winner, the
White Rose. We hear that the king has escaped and in a tear-jerking account, one Egbert tells of how
the queen fled, clutching her young treasure in her arms. Montague tells his men to let them go, as 'the
head is no good without the limbs', and victory is celebrated.

In the forest there is a cave and settlement where the outlaws live, now expecting to pick up some booty.
Margaret, showing the tender relationship she has with her young son, tries to cheer him up, explaining
how the forest will screen them. Enter the outlaw chief... Adeline's husband, Gondibert! He is so moved by
the queen's plight that the tables are turned; instead of his holding a sword over their heads, he leads them
to safety with Margaret following holding the sword over his head. To conclude the plot, Adeline, still in
disguise, asks to join Gondibert's band of outlaws; he tries to put her off by warning her what a hard life
it is, declaring how much he misses his family. All is revealed; the old retainer who had accompanied the
queen is brought in by a robber, and he looks forward to returning to a life less spectacular and hazardous.
The king, a non-person throughout the play, has fled to Edinburgh. Montague is trying to cut off Margaret's
retreat by sea with his forces near Dunstanburgh, but the queen goes through Cumbria instead with a
bodyguard provided by Gondibert. The play ends with a grand chorus of villagers. We considered that our
revival was sufficient, and none of us were keen to produce it as a full-scale opera.

So much for fact and myth. Some further literary sources now provide more insights into a sketchy
period of history – again with the most unusual or threatening episodes making the news. The peculiar
nature of the Border made life difficult enough, but religious conflicts, especially under the Tudors,
upset the local gentry. In 1515 Thomas Lord Dacre was Warden of the Middle March, of which Hexham
was part, and a letter from his servant to Archbishop Wolsey informed him that in his Regality of
Hexham there was trouble. People would not pay their rents and dues; two hundred people assembled
in Hexham to demand the release of prisoners in the gaol and eventually the authorities regained
control. Dacre 'caused their houses to be burnt in their own sight, for the more fearful example to other
offenders. And now they begin all to submit themselves.' He assured the archbishop that he would now
be able to collect the rents. (Hinds, 1896).

1. A wide view of Hexham from the air, looking from the south-west. On the far left are the railway and river. The Wentworth sports track is clear to the left, and the now-destroyed nuclear bunker, amid a spread of industry and retailers. The Sele is to the right centre, with Victorian and Edwardian terraces below. The light rectangular blocks are the old hospital at the east of the town.

2. Haugh Lane runs down the centre of the picture, past the cricket ground. Parallel are Market Street and Gilesgate. To the right are light industries, offices, houses, garages and retailers. The green places to the left are the Sele, Abbey Grounds and bowling green, with the Abbey at the bottom left.

3. Bottom left is the cricket ground, flanked on the right by Kingsgate, Queensgate and Eilansgate continuing as Haugh Lane to the railway bridge. Cockshaw and the Sele School are in the top-right hand corner.

4. The Abbey is in the top left corner; to the right are the Abbey Grounds, Sele, bowling green and Sele School. Centre, obliquely, is Market Street/Gilesgate to Holy Island, Eilansgate and Haugh Lane.

5. The Market Place in the 1820s: a painting by Henry Perlee Parker. (© Stan Beckensall and Hexham Abbey)

6. The east Market Place in the early nineteenth century: a popular reproduction of an etching by T. Allom.

7. Hexham Abbey from the north-west before the loss of the cedar tree and some of the blossom.

8. The Abbey from the south-west in February 2007.

9. The Queen's Hall in spring.

10. The war memorial in the Abbey Grounds.

11. The bandstand in autumn 2006.

12. The bandstand in winter. (© Michaela Long)

13. The bandstand at carnival time.

14. Folk Festival.

15. Festival children.

16. Festival Jazz.

17. Bowling green.

18. The swimming pool, once a wool warehouse.

19. The heron in the fountain.

20. Site of the tanneries.

21. The children's playground in February 2007.

22. The Golden Tapestry in the Abbey, February 2007.

Above: 23. Fifteenth-century depictions of Queen Etheldreda and Ecgfrith (?) to the rear of the organ, usually in dim light.

Opposite: 24. The Crown of Thorns panel from the fifteenth-century paintings in the north choir aisle.

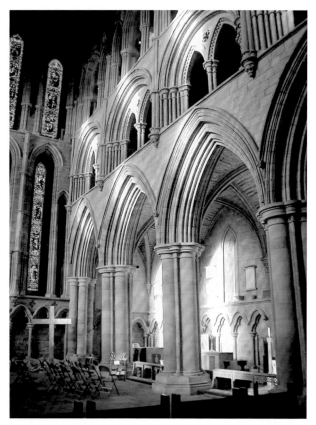

Left: 25. North transept arches.

Below: 26. The east aisle of the north transept.

27. The Annunciation.

28. The Visitation.

29. Abbey candlelight.

30. Abbey Festival.

A letter in 1522 from the Bishop of Carlisle to Wolsey said that, 'There is more theft and extortion by English thieves than there is by all the Scots of Scotland', and that Hexhamshire was the worst place, 'for in Exham (sic) itself every market day there is 80 or 100 strong thieves, and the poor men and gentlemen also see them which did rob them and their goods and dare neither complain of them by name nor say one word to them. They take all their cattle and horses, their corn as they carry it to sow or to the mill to grind, and at their houses bid them deliver what they will have or they shall be fired and burnt.' (Hinds, 1896). This picture is worth bearing in mind as we look at the Market Place today.

The Dissolution of the Monasteries

A fundamental change in Hexham resulted from the Dissolution of the Monasteries in 1536, when the power of the Priory came to an end, and the canons were expelled, with pensions. They did not give up easily, and when the king's commissioners came to carry out his command, we have the spectacle of their equipping themselves with weapons to resist, supported by many local people. We can now look at the day when Lionel Gray and Robert Collingwood came to 'dissolve' the Priory.

> They did see many persons assembled with bills, halberds and other defenceable weapons like men ready to defend a town in time of war. And in their passing the common bell of the town was rungen, and straight after the sound of it, the great bell of the monastery was likewise rung, whereby the people forceably assembled towards the monastery, where the said Lionel and Robert found the gates and doors fast shut. And a canon, called the Master of Ovingham, uttered these words: 'We be twenty brethren of this house, and we shall die ere that ye shall have this house'. The said Lionel and Robert said, 'Advise you well and speak with your brethren, and then give us answer finally'. And so the master departed into the house, and after his departure did come five or six the canons with divers other persons, like men of war in harness with swords girt about them, having bows and arrows and other weapons, and stood upon the tower and leads in the defence of their house, the said Lionel and Robert being without. About them did come and congregate many people, both men with weapons and many women. And so the said Lionel and Robert returned to meet the rest of the commissioners, and all together recoiled back to Corbridge, where they lay that night.

This was only a delay; in 1537 a royal army arrived, the Priory was dissolved and the canons were pensioned off or transferred to other duties. Carnaby, whose arms appear on a building to the west of the Abbey, was given the local lands and properties.

The effects of this episode were far-reaching. The town church, now incorporated in buildings on the south side of the Market, was by this time already decayed, with all kinds of buildings using it, so the only decent place of worship was the Priory. For this reason, the building was not stripped, but remained as the town church: otherwise we should not have the fine building there now. It was more than a church, though, as there was a whole range of monastic buildings to the west, with the cloister central to them. Many of these were eventually demolished, such as the refectory (dining room). The remains of the lavatorium (wash place) are still to be seen in the reconstructed west buildings that now house the courts and monastic workshop, and attached to these are what used to be the prior's house and garden, and outside the west door of the Abbey is a sixteenth-century block that includes the coat of arms of Sir Reginald Carnaby, who turned part of the external buildings into a house for himself, with the date 1539. The prior's house was rebuilt, a fine window surviving over the arch that leads past the Abbey administrative centre to the prior's garden and cloisters. Parts of these buildings are now social service offices, and to the south is a clinic.

The buildings have been subject to changes, especially in 1790 and after a fire in 1819, with a Dobson rebuilding. The Abbey since then has been subject to many changes, some of them rather vandalistic, but the remarkable thing is that so much fifteenth-century art has survived. How some of the paintings survived the Reformation is miraculous, for we have many images of fine quality of saints and bishops, and the misericords are splendid. Before the Dissolution the Priory was Roman Catholic, and those who wanted to worship in the old way had to find alternative buildings, even though this was forbidden. Later still the Nonconformist Churches were to grow and spread, but meanwhile the enforced changes in liturgy and philosophy must have been hard for some to bear.

A gentler era followed the accession of James I, although there were many cases of violence reported to the Manor Court. In 1761 a horrendous event marred the general peacefulness of the area. It is known as the Hexham Riot. The event has been researched recently by many historians, and what follows is summary of what happened. (Corfe, T., 2005)

The Hexham Riot, 1761

Local people were called to the Moothall where conscripts to the militia were to be chosen. This was a kind of selective National Service. Trouble was anticipated; troops were drafted to the Market Place 'in order to put a stop to riotous assemblies'. The local people refused to be balloted for military service. William Allen, an officer of the North Yorkshire Militia, described what happened as the situation became tense. He reported people packing into the town and insulting his troops.

He said of his men that 'they bore it with greatest coolness and moderation. At one o'clock, or a little after, the proclamation was read, and they were acquainted with the penalty if they did not disperse. They still continued to wave their monstrous sticks, clubs and quarter staffs in the most insolent manner, over the heads of our men, for by this time they had come within reach of our bayonets, with which our front rank charged, and soon after they made a vigorous effort upon our left and broke in upon them'. Shooting broke out, 'upon which the word of command was given to fire, as it became an act of necessity and self-defence'.

He described the aftermath of the slaughter: 'And now we had an opportunity of contemplating the bloody scene before us, twenty-four being left on the spot, eighteen of whom were dead and the rest dangerously wounded'. The next day was wet, 'which was of service, as it washed the remains of yesterday out of the Market Place'. Fifty-two civilians were killed and forty-four wounded. A warrant was issued for the arrest of seventeen others in connection with the riot.

When Peter Patterson of Shilvington was tried for High Treason and found guilty, they wrote of him as 'one of 500 persons and upwards armed and arrayed in a warlike manner' who 'waged and levied public war against our lord the King'. He was seventy-three. He was drawn upon a hurdle to the place of execution in Morpeth. He stated that he did not think the crime he had committed was worthy of death. He survived falling off the cart with the rope around his neck when the rope broke. A new rope was found, while he waited. He was hanged again, cut down, drawn and quartered.

The longest survivors of the riot were Samuel Carter and Cornelius Ridley. Samuel was lamed for life, and his mother, Sarah, pregnant at the time, was killed in the riot. He made spinning wheels, and died in 1825. Cornelius Ridley, twelve at the time of the riot, was shot through the mouth and became a cordwainer, dying in 1828. Both men were respected Hexham citizens and leading figures in the Independent Church.

The reader is left to evaluate this serious address preached in the Abbey church to the common people:

A reenactment of the Hexham Riot in the Market Place. (Colin Dallison)

O foolish People and unwise! How unmindful are you of the rich Blessings of Providence? How ungrateful to the best of kings and the mildest administration? How little have YOU felt the miseries of war? Alas! I fear your very Prosperity makes you wanton; your very Liberty tempts you to be licentious. You are apparently discontented with your low situation in life, and therefore begin to hate and envy all in authority. Do but turn impartial eyes back upon your late Behaviour: how inconsistent was it with the amiable character of BRITONS?

How contrary to every appearance of loyal subjects? And how unworthy the Behaviour of reasonable Men; but much more of sober CHRISTIANS?

What infatuation could move you to such daring, such Treasonable Attempts? Many of you vainly imagine, perhaps, that you mean no harm; nor did you go with any bad or bloody designs. But did your presence give countenance to this MAD and WICKED action? The Militia Law, you say, is a very bad one, and therefore ought to be repealed. How? Are YOU the only proper and infallible judges of what is or is not expedient for the Good and Well-being of the whole community? How came men of your rank by this extraordinary knowledge? Matters of state are much above you.

Repent of your Folly. Let this be a severe warning to you. Meddle not hereafter with things above your capacity. Be Humble and Content. And if our gracious sovereign shall think fit, out of mere mercy and tenderness, to make but A FEW EXAMPLES among you, for such a daring, heinous crime, be you that escape ever duly thankful for the great and undeserved lenity shown towards you.

Clearly, the history of this event was mainly written by those who were considered to be the victors.

Like other towns, Hexham has since then celebrated many national events, such as a huge gathering in the Market Place to proclaim King George V as king in 1910, or street parties in 1918 to celebrate the end of the First World War and the 1935 Silver Jubilee, but the Hexham Riot has struck a particular chord today, with recent enactments in the place where it happened. It may become a permanent feature in town life. War plays a big part in people's memories, and the memorial to those who died particularly in two world wars has attracted not only a continuation of respect for the dead at annual ceremonies but, perhaps even more poignantly, a book on Hexham war memorials by Alan Grint which traces the lives and deaths of local people in the First World War – a very important piece of research. It is the thoroughness of this work that makes it unnecessary for me to try to add to it.

Chapter 3

Earning A Living

If you enter Hexham from the north over the river and rail bridges you will be aware of the extensive wood-chip industry of Egger. It has caused adverse comment since its construction on account of fires and smoke, and of the way it has been allowed to grow so big, dominating the approach from the east. Some think it is logical that in a part of Britain where so much timber is grown commercially there should be a factory to process its products. The question is always… where? It brings jobs and income to the town, being a producer of large quantities of chipboard. This factory is only one sign of many changes in the Tyne valley, for where there used to be extensive market gardens are now small-scale industries and retailers. The car, as usual, accounts for many of these changes, and the use of the car allows the growth of such out-of-town retailers as Tesco, Aldi and Waitrose. Among the factories is the very important winner of a Queen's Award for Industry, Multichem, a home-grown enterprise which has developed specialised inks. It is characteristic of the North East as a whole that manufacturing has declined enormously, and worryingly, and that retailing and office blocks thrive. In many places now covered with new buildings lie the remnants of old industries such as fell-mongering, leather-making, small-scale iron works and market-gardening that once provided a living for hundreds of people.

This chapter will consider what is still visible of some of these industries, mostly concentrated in the north of the town, between the market and the river. Here the land is low-lying and crossed by streams which played an important part in industry.

Tanning and associated industries

A centre of the tanning industry is an area known as Cockshaw. Although the town centre with its Abbey and other old buildings tends to be well known, visitors may not be aware of the great interest that Cockshaw has in building up a picture of Hexham's livelihood, an interest which extends from a look at its existing buildings to a search in sources such as documents and old photographs for the fascinating story of hundreds of people whose names seldom reach the history books. It is an opportunity to see how many themes intertwine.

Cockshaw is a name first recorded in 1296, meaning a ridge where there were game cocks or wild birds. An oil painting shows the Abbey and other town buildings rising above the burn, with haymakers on its slopes; the burn itself has steep-roofed cottages built alongside. The burn defines the west edge of the town, seen flowing under the bridge near 'The Fox' in a steep valley which is being landscaped in an extensive new drainage project. At first there are private gardens flanking it close to the bridge, and the garden of one of them, Tynedale Terrace, has a seventeenth-century doorway taken from St Mary's Chare inserted as its back door. The other door of the pair is still in the Chare, but has crossed the road. As the burn enters the Cockshaw road, it is spanned by a small metal bridge known as the Sele Bridge, as it leads there. Close by is an old square stone 'pant', which used to be one of the main sources of clean water here.

The road flanking, and leading to, the burn has an interesting array of houses, including one with a 1688 date known as the Priest's House, as it originally was part of the Roman Catholic church and house. There is a mixture of styles and periods, with Dunwoodie Terrace being built of small random sandstones that look brick-sized, some with their original nineteenth-century timber door-casings with a projecting canopy, facing the brick-faced Ordley Terrace, which may be much older. Cockshaw Terrace has seen many recent changes; although some Victorian stone houses remain on either side of the Priest's House, part of the terrace was demolished, to be replaced with modern stone-fronted houses that are in keeping with the area, and a rather ugly chapel was also demolished to make way for stone and brick houses.

The whole of this area has been redeveloped, and courtyards and terraces now stand in places where there used to be industries. It has been plagued by flooding, as the picture shows, but the drainage scheme has not only alleviated that but produced an interesting feature, for the 'flood' wall carries carved names for 'water' in many languages, the stream bed has been cobbled and landscaped, and Heraclitus' dictum that 'You cannot step in the same river twice' stares out from the bed. Another splendid touch is a flat part of the wall amid the rounded tops which declares, 'no inhabitants in or about this burn shall wash their puddings in Cockshaw Burn. (1660-2006)'.

In 1661 it was ordered that, 'no inhabitants in or about this town shall wash any puddings in the west burn called the Abbey Garth Burn or the Cockshaw Burn, or shall wash any filthy things in either of the same burns until they come to George Leadbitter's house being the nethermost house in the town upon pain of 6s 8d'. By 'puddings' they meant animal intestines, and the limit of the town is here defined as a house that we assume to be on the site of the present Ordley Terrace. The fine, for that time, was a hefty one, but this did not seem to deter many people, as the practice continued, as we see in the mid-nineteenth-century health reports.

At the same time there were regulations to prevent tanners and glovers from emptying their 'lime pits, dubs and baits betwixt four o'clock in the morning and five in the afternoon upon pain of 6s 8d'. One can imagine the problems in the summer when there was less flow of water. Other rules aimed at limiting the cleaning of pits to the autumn when there was more rain, but this too was flouted. The problems continued throughout the eighteenth century and into the next. So what was it about this industry that was so repulsive?

Fortnightly stock markets from March to November were followed by local butchery, some around the Market Place. More skins and hides were brought in when there was good transport along the Tyne valley. Some materials, such as alum, came from Ravenscar. Oak bark was needed, locally from coppiced oak, and the 1826 map shows a windmill on Tyne Green for crushing it. By 1889 the Hextol Tannery was importing 400 tonnes of bark yearly from Belgium and Holland. There was plenty of lime locally to loosen and remove hair, fat and wool, but chemicals used to prevent the skins from putrefying and producing awful smells. The essential use of water led to regulations from the fourteenth century onwards demanding that the siting of the tanneries be downstream from the town, away from drinking water supplies.

By law the leather trades were separated into 'Tanners and Shoemakers' and 'Skinners and Glovers'. Tanning was preceded by trimming and washing, the removal of hair and fat; the hides were soaked in substances that included dog muck and bird droppings, then given a final wash. It then all went to the pits, usually 6ft x 4ft (1.83m x 1.22m), separated by narrow walkways. Beginning with infusions of bark and

The area from the bowling green (bottom centre) and the cricket ground (top) contains what used to be a major tanning area and the site of a small iron foundry. The road to the right is Haugh Lane, becoming Eilansgate. Centre is recent housing. Kingsgate Terrace leads towards the bowling green from the left. The Sele and Sele School are in the bottom left-hand corner. Market Street/Gilesgate runs from the centre bottom of the picture to join Haugh Lane and Alexander Place.

A painting of Cockshaw, with the Sele and Abbey Grounds above the burn.

'The Priest's House', 1688.

Cockshaw Terrace today.

The Cockshaw Burn in flood. This is behind Holy Island House; the chapel to the right and the houses have been demolished and new ones built.

water, the skins were taken to pits where the mixtures were stronger, and the process lasted from nine to eighteen months, until at the end of the nineteenth century it was speeded up by the use of chromic salts.

Smoothing, drying in sheds with louvered windows (still to be seen) produced 'crust' leather, sealed by a guild official and sold to be made into shoes, saddles, harnesses, and belting. Shoemakers and saddlers had their shops nearby. The processing liquids were saved, and any flooding of the pits was an expensive disaster.

Skinners and glovers were involved in another branch of the industry. Skinners dealt in skins of sheep, lamb, goat, kid and deer, processed by a 'Tawyer' (skin dresser), this time using alum, salt, fats and fish oils. They were soaked in lime, stretched and scraped, and fermented for weeks in a vat. The dried skins were then sold to glovers and others who made soft leather goods. Sheep dealers were also 'fellmongers', which meant that they sold cleaned wool to the cloth trade.

The remains of these industries, though faint, are still there, but Hexham was most famous for its gloves. In the Cockshaw area alone are two gloveries marked on the 1853 map, and historically gloves were so important that they were even left in people's wills. 'The Hexham Tans' (after which a café is now named) were of soft leather coloured with ochre, one local source being at High Shield, south of the town, provided by a yellow Fell clay, though Dutch ochre was preferred. At its height, the industry

The site of the tanneries is preserved, with Henry Bell's office and others made from a variety of materials.

employed over 1,100 people working from home to sew the cut-outs. In 1822 there were eleven glove manufacturers, and 23,504 dozen pairs of gloves were produced annually. Two of the glove manufacturers operated in Cockshaw.

The decline and death of the industry by the end of the nineteenth century came largely as a result of the switch to factories in big cities. This is a snapshot of the processes at work. Part of what is now covered over is shown in an auction sale of 1830 of a tanyard and house there, with '52 tan pits, 2 drying houses, a good bark mill and loft, 1 ring wheel and a hay loft'. The man who bought them was Henry Bell, whose office is still there, whose family wool factory is now the swimming pool, and who donated the bandstand to the town.

Large-scale maps show us exactly where these tanneries were. We shall return to Holy Island after we have followed the burns north to the River Tyne, to look at more industrial sites. The stream skirts Holy Island on its west, then, after culverting under the road, emerges again as a stream which flows past a garage for specialised cars ('The Horseless Carriage'), behind which is the site of another iron foundry. The house attached to this has been recently restored, and some of the industrial buildings are still standing. Opposite there was, until recently, a large gasometer, with some of its low stone buildings and round-topped windows still there.

Further north is yet another mixture of old and new: a bus depot stands beside the House of Correction, opposite which the burn passes under two arches under a restored old building with slatted windows. This was once part of a large tannery, extending to the east, later to be covered by the West Cumbria Farmers' warehouse, which in turn was demolished to make way for some attractive stone and brick offices and houses, including some 'affordable' housing. West Cumbria Farmers is still represented there on reduced premises catering for the needs of modern farming. A fertiliser works had been built at Tyne Green on this site in 1859, and extended in 1889 to use the bones from the tanning industry.

The burns are culverted again under Ridley Terrace (dated 1864), passing under the railway line, then emptying into the Tyne through more elaborate culverting, joining another small stream at the golf course. These boundaries mark the western extent of tanning, and now end the new spread along the Haugh (flat alluvial land) to Egger in the east, a fundamental recent change from a time not long ago when market gardens were the norm.

A tannery building on Tyne Green
Road.

We can now return along Burn Lane, cross the road towards the town centre, past red-brick houses which replaced slums, and meet the tip of Holy Island, marked by a water outlet known as the Glover's Pant (opposite the remains of a stone glovery) that was built in 1858 after the Public Health report. It is at the gable end of a stone house that has a date-stone reading K/TB 1757; to the rear it has the line of a stone external staircase. It adjoins Holy Island House, which is one of the oldest and finest in Hexham. It has a date on the lintel, but one has to be careful with these, as they can be added to commemorate a special event. It reads 1637, with a K, which almost certainly stands for Kirsopp, as that family owned it as late as 1860, and an Alderman of the Skinners' and Glovers' Society, of that name, lived there in 1741. It is also one of the earliest Mass Houses in Hexham, where Catholics were officially not tolerated but a blind eye was turned on their private worship. A small room at the south end of the first floor was a chapel, with the priest's bedroom above it. The house was sold by the last Kirsopp to live there to a tanner, who lived there until 1910; was lived in until 1959, and then used as a warehouse, store and office by a master plumber. Since then the house has been gradually renovated by owners who are knowledgeable and careful, so it remains one of Hexham's outstanding buildings, in the Elizabethan style. It is double-fronted, and the beams that tie the walls together can be seen end-on from the outside. The roof has six bays, with two gables and a steeply-pitched slate roof, with chimneys at the two gable ends.

Two lines of windows face the road, all square-headed, and it is clear from their surrounds that the upper windows and those on the lower floor have all been changed. To make an attractive horizontal division, 'string courses' of stone have been inserted. The pavement outside the front of the house is higher than the doorstep. Originally the stream would have flowed past, until the road which had little bridges over it was culverted and became a higher road surface. Here the windows are of a different order from those above, like closely-packed rectangles. The inside, too, is very interesting, but I shall not go into detail as the house is private.

Behind the house were the tanneries, and there is an external stone stair from ground level. There is a row of attractive houses facing Holy Island House across Gilesgate, one of which included a small shop, the brickwork of which has been well cleaned and renovated. At the time of writing, its neighbour is being stripped of cement rendering to reveal fine large sandstone blocks, then the road up the hill shows where buildings have been demolished or reused, including a car park. The whole area is a mixture of

The 1858 pant at the north end of Holy Island.

ancient and modern, of narrow lanes, brick and stone buildings, some with warehouse-type openings. Among them is the site of a destroyed nineteenth-century chapel and facing 'The Old Tannery' is a strange-looking building that was a Methodist Chapel.

The chapel was built when a split occurred in the Methodist congregation in Hexham, a small group of Free Methodists establishing themselves here in 1859. In one of its lives it became a shop. The third Methodist church in the area, at what is now Tanners Row, included a school, was put up for sale in 1900, not sold, used as a Mission Hall for the Wesleyans, bought as a furniture store and used as such until 1972, then demolished. In a town the size of Hexham it is interesting to see so many places of worship, their uses and reuses. More will be said about this later.

Another accompaniment to working life was drink, and there are two public houses side by side, one still in use. What is now called 'The Old Tannery' still has its original name inscribed in stone: 'The Skinners' Arms'. It is a splendid example of turn of the nineteenth century building, dated 1897, with patterned glossy brick and decorative sandstone, similar to 'The Grapes' in Back Street. Adjoining it, hardly recognisable as a pub, is 'The Tanners'. Apparently, fights between drinkers from the two were once a common feature of Saturday nights. The stream from the tannery runs beside the pub, with Glovers' Place on the other side, and this provides one way in to the main tannery area today.

What you see now is the result of the clearance of many of the working areas such as tan pits and processing shops, with sufficient remaining to give a sense of place and the scale of the industry. Much has been recorded by a *Hexham Courant* photographer, the late Hilton Edgar. The last major owners and managers of leather working, fellmongering and wool grading were the Bells. It was Henry Bell who built the wool warehouse which now provides the front for the town swimming pool. He supplied sheep and lamb skins to the glove trade, including a glovery of his own on the site, but when glove-making ceased at the end of the nineteenth century the pelts were sold elsewhere in the country. His two sons developed the fellmongering/woolstapling side of the business. Until its closure in 1975 it operated as a

Holy Island House, 1657.

The tannery area is to the left of Gilesgate and to the right of the Sele School and its playground. Gilesgate Place and Holy Island are at the bottom of the picture, the Halgut Burn running under the roads, but the Cockshaw Burn is open to the right. Glovers' Place, a redundant chapel, The Old Tannery and The Tanner's Arms are visible. To the left of Gilesgate, from the bottom, are Circle Place, a car park, the Community Centre and the swimming pool on the site of the wool warehouse. (Courtesy of Terry Robson)

skin yard, to which sheepskins came in weekly from abattoirs in Gateshead, Carlisle and Stockton. The skins were inspected, soaked, and passed through a washing machine. Any extra water needed came from the well on a continuous chain of buckets. The skins were stretched on a conveyor belt, lime and sodium sulphide were applied to dissolve the hair root, the wool was then pulled and sorted by hand over a curved wooden beam. It would then be dried, sorted and baled. During the Second World War some of the best pelts were sent to make flying jackets.

The site closed in 1975, and was rescued from dereliction by Terry Robson in 1977. As you stand on the stone floor today by the stream, or look down from a wooden walkway, you are faced with an amazing group of multi-period buildings of different materials, changed, but still retaining some of their original functions. Henry Bell's office is still there, the curved window of his stairway overlooking the

Display panel at the Tanners' Yard. (Courtesy of Hexham Historic Partnership)

yard, the links between some buildings as wooden structures have been retained, and what remains has been turned over to quite different use as offices, but Terry Robson, whose electrical business once occupied much of the site, is the one who made it possible.

Four guilds have already been mentioned, and played an important part in the government of Hexham. In addition to the Tanners', Shoemakers', Skinners', and Glovers', there were Hatters' and Weavers'. There are few records of these. There were rules about meetings, and rules about fines for misconduct, and the fact that these fines were divided equally between the Manor Court and the guilds suggests that they were working closely together. Anna Rossiter (1996, 2005) has researched documents of the seventeenth and eighteenth centuries and shown how leather workers were not only an important sector of the town's population but were dominant in its government. It was, unlike Morpeth or Alnwick, never a borough, but the guilds were important. The most interesting documentary evidence is a transcript of a photocopy of a document donated to The County Record Office in 1973, with no record of where it came from: such is the importance of a chance find. It is dated to 1732 and concerns the shoemakers, and supports previous research which shows that in the seventeenth century they were the largest occupational group with something like 141 members. Sixty-five were buried between 1650 and 1700, and in 1732 there were 126 signatures to their 'Articles, Rules and Orders to be Observed and kept by the Society of Shoemakers in Hexham'. They were not particularly well-off, compared with tanners. The club was broken up in 1871, so it had a long life.

People allowed to join the club were elected by majority vote, had to be above forty years old, and healthy in body and mind. Wives were only allowed in to pay their husbands' dues. Money was collected at each meeting by stewards, and fines were levied for such offences as non-attendance, drinking, smoking, gambling and trade malpractice. In return it acted as a Friendly Society, helping people in times of sickness and trouble. The articles and rules are published by Hexham Local History Society (*Hexham Historian*, No. 15, 2005), and include clauses such as this, dated 1765: 'At the Death of any Member, everyone in this club shall pay the first meeting after his death six-pence towards clearing the funeral expenses'. The closure of the club is marked by: 'The Club was broken up on September 1st 1871, and divided 121 pounds among 24 members'. But who were these people living in Hexham, and where did they come from?

The census returns are vital. The original census of 1801 was confined to buildings, the number of people and broad employment categories, until in 1841 it became a truly national census with names, ages and occupations. In the Cockshaw area we see the lives of people vividly in the period 1841-91, a time of rapid national change. Buildings were demolished and new ones built. In 1891 we see Cockshaw spreading up the hill to Millfield, Dunwoodie Terrace, Hamilton Terrace, and a block called Brookside appears. This was, however, in the period after the tanning industry declined; its period of being the largest employer was the seventeenth, eighteenth and early nineteenth centuries. The Industrial Revolution which transformed the North East was based largely on the mineral wealth of the area. Coal was supreme; there were widespread deposits, the finest concentrated near the coast, and small local industries at first benefited from these. There was also some local iron, but some of the most important minerals included lead: the Pennine area became the world's largest producer of lead for a while.

The Cockshaw survey discovered that about a third of Hexham's population was born elsewhere. Many came from villages in Northumberland, Durham and Cumbria. After the catastrophic famine in Ireland, thirty-three people in Cockshaw were born there in 1861 and twenty in 1871. In 1881, 258 people in this area out of 374 were born in Hexham and 116 elsewhere (*Hexham Historian* Vol. 4).

One very interesting aspect of the census is what jobs people did. Our report itemised cadgers, linen-weavers, cow-keepers, appraisers, hawkers, wool-carders, hatters, tinsmiths, whitesmiths, straw-bonnet makers, mendicants, lead-ore washers, chimney sweeps, a keeper of prisons (unemployed), and washerwomen. Many Cockshaw men and women worked in the market gardens. All these occupations were in addition to the leather industry workers, which by this time was almost dead. Job losses in that industry were offset by an increase in the number of painters, florists, grocers, drapers, stone masons, butchers, mail-cart drivers, dressmakers and domestic servants, just to name a few. The growth of railways also absorbed more labour. The building trade increased in prosperity and more people were employed in transport. Not many people were unemployed.

Many people retired much later than they do today, and lived in the same house or area. As for the children, the Education Act of 1870 demanded that School Boards should cater for the children. Whereas in 1861 only 66 of the children were classed as 'scholars' in the Cockshaw area, by 1871 the number was up to 101 (83 in 1881). Today, Cockshaw retains fascinating relics of its industrial past, and despite the attraction of the Abbey and its grounds, this area provides us with an insight into how most of the people in the past made their living. Changes in the use of land and buildings in the area reflect changes in social and industrial conditions, and much of this has now been mapped and documented.

Chapter 4

Conditions Of Life: Health and Sanitation

What is now a clean and attractive market town has not always been so. It is not only the crowding together of people that makes good sanitation and clean water vital; if there are industries which produce waste and by their nature undermine the health of the people and if there is a further influx of people attracted by the possibility of making a living, sanitary and other provisions have to keep pace. That means that local authorities have to be capable of coping with these problems if the health and wellbeing of the people are not to suffer.

A detailed, fascinating insight into conditions in small Northumberland towns is given in a series of Public Health reports in the mid-nineteenth century that mark the movement away from leaving all matters of public health to local authorities and individuals to some sort of central state control. Overcrowding in industrial towns, filth, disease and moral disintegration alarmed even those who were insulated from such privation themselves. There were great souls who looked in detail at what was happening around them, whose consciences would not let them rest, and who came out of their safe, protected lives to work for their fellow human beings. Prison reform, anti-slavery, votes for a wider range of people, the fight against disease and poverty, the improvement of living and working conditions were all great causes. Lord Shaftsbury, Florence Nightingale and Josephine Butler were among those who fought for a better quality of life for those who could only express themselves by their frustration. Churches took on the fight, some managing to break away from the cosy respectability of established religion. Methodists and Quakers and other dissenters reached the parts of society that others were afraid to enter. Clergymen and doctors working among the poor, often at great risk to their own health, saw what had to be done through radical change.

There were, of course, the fat cats who preferred things to go on as before because they were the main beneficiaries of the exploitation of other human beings. Some ratepayers were reluctant to pay out money towards the improvement of the living conditions of the poor. They saw the problems of an influx of vagrants, Irish itinerant labour and other unsavoury beings as an added financial burden. They had to be convinced that if conditions of health through better sanitation, water supply and housing were to improve that it would in the end actually cost them less in poor relief. In some Northumberland towns there may have been a kind of mafia of self-interest that wanted things left as they were. 'The rich man in his castle, the poor man at his gate' was for some the natural order of things, for 'God made them high and lowly'.

The Government's response to the enormous problems of the nation was to send inspectors to places where they were invited. They were to report on health by gathering together the opinions of all those who had a voice in the community and by seeing for themselves what sort of conditions people lived

A rare source of spring water
close to Cockshaw Burn.

in. The spread of disease, especially cholera and typhus was the trigger, for disease and death were no respecters of persons. The inspection would offer practical assessments on how conditions could be improved, and for how much money. It was then up to the local government to decide whether they should wish the Act to apply to them, which meant central support for their improvements.

The name stamped on the report of inspections is that of Robert Rawlinson, who was to report to the General Board of Health in London. In the mid-nineteenth century the great concern expressed by many for the health and welfare of so many British people found its voice in Parliament. The result was increasing central intervention, and in particular the establishment of a General Board of Health. It was not just the new industrial towns that bred disease; the countryside was clearly not the healthy place that rosy-cheeked, vibrant milkmaids seemed to epitomise.

The procedure for applying the Public Health Act to any area was to get 10 per cent of the ratepayers to ask for an enquiry, at which interested parties could have their say. Although it was quite obvious that conditions of life were insanitary for many, those rich enough to be ratepayers were reluctant to part with their money, and were wary of a central authority interfering with their rights to administer their own local affairs. In the examples that I have chosen, the story of inspections and what they revealed becomes very clear.

The Market Place, as we have seen, was surrounded by a mass of buildings that included pigsties, slaughterhouses and privies, built partly over the canonical cemetery. It was Rawlinson's report that filled in so many details not only about the centre of Hexham, but about conditions in adjoining areas, especially Cockshaw. There was Hexham's main industry – tanning – and particularly the manufacturing of gloves (known as Hexham Tans). Recent work by Anna Rossiter added considerably to the picture of the seventeenth century (about which very little work has been done), and David Jennings' research took him into a consideration of public health later than the Rawlinson report.

Many of the same themes that appear in reports on other small towns are echoed in the Hexham document, with some interesting additions. The report was published in 1853. The enquiry took place after 152 people had requested it (out of a population of 2,982). We are told that notice was given via the press and by fixing notices to the doors of churches and chapels. The report gave a brief history and accounts of the geology and meteorology. The relevance of rainfall to drainage and sewerage was pointed out. An account of the modern town showed it to be crowded, unplanned, dirty and 'not conducive to the health of the inhabitants'. More detail followed. The report says that in the Market Place:

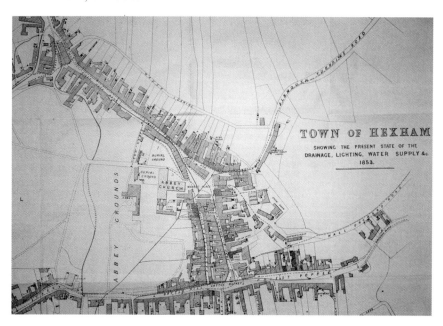

The 1853 map which accompanied Rawlinson's report.

On the west and north no conveniences at all exist, not one inch of ground to use as a yard…In one instance the entire refuse of a family is deposited in a cellar immediately beneath the post office, so that the whole town is brought within range of its infectious influence…On the south and east sides of the Market-place are to be found, in the generality of cases, small yards containing an area 5 or 6 feet square, and having ashpit and privy. On all sides the yards are surrounded by high walls, so that however much the wind may blow without, within the contaminated precincts no breeze ever comes.

Yet the lie of the land, sloping down to the river, should have made good drainage possible. A local sanitary report summed up the situation: 'Hexham, although possessing every natural advantage for cleanliness and healthfulness, has, by its construction, been rendered comparatively filthy and unhealthy'.

If the area immediately around the market was bad, Gilligate (Gilesgate) was worse. Several groups of houses had no privies, and those that did were shared by many families, no one taking responsibility for keeping them clean. A particular horror is described there:

In one instance the drainage from a piggery, privy and ashpit has found its way into the room of an adjoining house, and liquid oozes through the wall, and runs down from the second to the first floor, in such quantity as to wet the beds. A well has been sunk in the room several feet deep, in which these pestiferous drainings are allowed to accumulate until it is full, and then they are removed to make way for more.

Where there were drains, as at Black Bull Bank (now the road with The Forum Cinema in it) the five drains that opened onto it formed a stagnant pool at the bottom. 'The structures intended for drains are, except in very wet weather, reservoirs, so that almost constantly, from every opening, but especially from those in the vicinity of a water-closet, exhale very offensive and injurious effluvia'. No wonder 'the sanitary condition of Hexham is of the lowest class. The few attempts that have been made to improve it, have been too paltry and unconnected to be of much use; they have been made for individual rather than for public good, hence their inutility, and in many instances ultimate injuriousness'.

There had been an epidemic of smallpox that 'afforded ample proof that in overcrowded and low damp houses in the neighbourhood of offal heaps, disease finds its most numerous victims, and there operates with the most deadly effect'. In one house with forty people living there, thirteen caught smallpox and twelve of these cases were from two families. At the end of Fore Street, one of today's main shopping streets, there were ten cases near to a yard where 'slaughterhouses, piggeries, dung-heaps, stagnant putrid pools, and all the other filthy concomitants are crowded together beneath the windows of a row of houses that are parallel therewith'. The market, being a focal point for agricultural trade, included beasts, and in addition to a large number of slaughterhouses was the meat market, still known as 'The Shambles', in the town centre.

One would imagine that the local doctors would have linked disease to such bad conditions, but there are instances (especially when cholera came to Sunderland in the 1830s, later to spread all over Britain with devastating results) when local practitioners denied the link. Why? Sometimes financial considerations – anything that interfered with trade or anything that was going to cost more in taxes made some people close their eyes.

One surgeon, Thomas Jefferson, who had seen only one case of cholera in 1831 and 1832, admitted there 'is generally more or less fever', but no more than anywhere else, and 'thinks if the Public Health Act was in force, the sanitary condition of the town could not be improved'. Mr Robert Stokoe, who had practised for forty years and was the senior surgeon in Hexham, admitted epidemics of smallpox and scarlet fever, but added that, 'I have always considered the town healthy, being seldom visited with contagious or infectious diseases, and never of long duration'. He considered that proof of this was that people came to stay in Hexham for their health. He blamed local deaths on 'the influx of sick strangers', thought that the mortality figures had been taken from selected periods when disease was rife, and said that the smallpox prevailed among the unvaccinated. William Angus Temperley, a corn merchant, countered with: 'If the town is so healthy as they describe, the average mortality ought to be lower'.

Mr Thomas Stainthorpe, surgeon and medical officer to the Union, 'Considers the town very unhealthy. Attended 217 cases of smallpox during the last winter'. He proved his point by producing statistics to show where smallpox was prevalent in the winter of 1851 and 1852. He arranged the statistics into the five administrative 'wards' of Hexham. Gilligate had ninety-six cases, and this area included the crowded tannery areas of Cockshaw and Tyne Green. Priestpopple (originally the land owned by priests) had forty-one; Market Street and the Market Place area had twenty-five cases. Hencotes (including Back Street, Battle Hill, Victoria Place and West Spital Cottage) had thirty-four cases. The Hexham Union Workhouse had twenty cases. All told, this made 216. Of the seventy-one cases of fever, Gilligate had thirty-four during the past two and a half years. He also mentioned that in 1849, five or six cases of Asiatic cholera occurred in Hexham, and the situation was saved by a general meeting of townspeople that arranged for food, bed and bodily clothing.

In view of the adverse reports on Hexham, it is difficult to understand why anyone should have been against making the changes proposed to improve the cleanliness of the town and for providing it with an adequate supply of clean water. There seemed to be more opposition in Hexham to change than in other towns; 302 people signed against it, and of these 188 were from Gilesgate! The reasons they gave were:

There are no less than sixteen public and open pants and fountains in the town, constantly supplied with a sufficient quantity of water; and, together with the supply of water from private pumps, is more than adequate.

The town of Hexham, from its peculiar situation, has always been, and still is, unquestionably one of the most healthy towns in the kingdom.

The nuisances from time to time recurring in the town, and any want of sanitary regulations, are amply provided against by the powers vested in the Board of Guardians and other local authorities, the said nuisances being in themselves comparatively insignificant.

We further find, that many of the parties signing the petition to the general board of health were, by the propositions held out at that time, led to believe that the measure was one of a trifling nature.

To summarise: Hexham is one of the healthiest places to live, there is plenty of fresh water, we can cope with nuisances ourselves, and you people who signed the petition didn't know what expense you were letting yourselves in for.

The report on Hexham has more detail than many other towns, including details of the gasworks. Other reports include the burial of the dead. Today the main burial grounds used at the time of the report have been landscaped. A walk from the Market Place past the Abbey on the north side has a raised area to the north where most of the town's dead were buried, but is now without the mass of gravestones. A sub-committee reported that if each grave were allowed to occupy 6ft of space, there was room for 1,965 graves. The population entitled to use the space was 5,528. The average number of burials per year was 120, and if this continued it meant that each grave would have to be reopened every fifteen years or even less to bury more bodies:

It is indeed often very unpleasant to witness the remains of bodies dug out of the ground before they have become sufficiently decomposed. Until three or four years ago the usual depth of the graves was on 3 feet, so that the top of the coffins would be scarcely 2 feet from the surface, a circumstance which could not but prove injurious to the health of the inhabitants residing in the immediate vicinity of the churchyard.

They changed the practice and made the depth of the grave 5ft.

Of more concern was the 'custom, still resorted to by some families, of making use of the inside of the church as a place of interment...there are nearly fifty families which have availed themselves of this privilege during a comparatively recent period of time'. The issue was not straightforward, as people wanted to be buried near their relatives and regarded this as their right irrespective of the danger that it posed. The solution was that a new graveyard had to be found, and that no one should be buried in the church.

People found bones strewn around the burial ground – this still happens when any excavation work is being done in that part of Hexham which the Market Street houses back on to. Another burial ground was in the place now occupied by the Abbey nave, where poorer people were buried. Since 1850 there must have been many bones of all periods disturbed, removed, dumped or reburied with the various rebuildings and modifications made to the Abbey.

Water supply was examined in detail, as this was a crucial factor in the spread of disease. The inspectors did not think that Hexham had paid enough attention to it. The old pant-head system had been in existence since 1800, without providing sufficient or clean enough water. Pants, wells and pumps together provided 36,000 gallons, or 8 gallons a day per person. This was less than Nottingham, Liverpool or Hartlepool. Less than 8 gallons was actually available because much of it escaped from the pants. If a service pipe were made available, all the supply could be used.

The quality of the water was also poor, and the pant-head supplies could only be used for washing. The water had to be purified, for near the source of the supply were brick and tile works pouring muddy refuse into the burn. Further on were fields with cattle: more pollution. It thus reached the pants unfiltered: 'It cannot but be wondered at that a town pretending, and not without reason, to a considerable amount of intelligence, should have so long allowed itself of an all-important necessary of life to be furnished by such rude, absurd, and vicious methods'. Wow!

They found that sudden showers made the water unusable in the pants; the one in Gilligate had a deposit of four inches of mud. The answer to this was house-service at high pressure through a public waterworks, and that would cost only a little more than the present unregulated system. The old committee had to go, although they had done their best with 'a bad system and small funds'. The construction of a reservoir above the town was proposed, and the harnessing of water supplies in springs could add to the water flowing through main pipes. (One of the springs remains just beside the Cockshaw Burn today). As for the pants, the inspectors were not insisting on their closure, but pointed out that other towns had got rid of them because they encouraged servants and others to congregate there!

From time to time when modern building work is undertaken, a little more of Hexham's history is revealed. On one occasion when a large house was being underpinned at the entrance to the Wentworth complex, a well appeared. A similar one appeared at Corbridge in the garden of a house and the latest was to the south of the town, again in a garden, overlooking the Middle School field. From the plan of the town that is included with the report, there are many wells marked, representing many private water supplies.

A perspective

Sometimes the meaning of much of history is lost. It becomes a matter of words and of juggling ideas, putting forward theories, being clever. We may speak of disease as something remote, but when we are reminded of what it implies for the people suffering it, it may become real – even from a distance. Take cholera, for example – a word that appears in all the above reports. What did it mean to those who experienced it? Its terrible reality was that it began with a sensation of giddiness, unease, anxiety, followed by 'prodigious evacuation, when the whole intestines seem to be emptied at once'. There was a fluttering in the pit of the stomach, tightness of the waist. Limbs became clammy and the heart slowed down. Movement made the sufferer sick. The lining of the intestines came away in motions that were like rice water. The body lost water in a great purge, shrivelling the victim. Cramps followed, with pains like acute arthritis. The features collapsed and the body turned blue or black. Pain could contract the person into a ball, and they stayed like that until death.

The sheer inability of anyone in authority, including surgeons, to deal with this was understandable, but the absurd quackery that accompanied diagnoses and treatment was often delivered by pompous, self-seeking fools. What the sensible realised at the time was that the conditions under which disease flourished could be rectified. It was this kind of desperate situation that formed the background to Edwin Chadwick's report, presented to the House of Lords in 1842: *Report on the Sanitary Conditions of the Labouring Population of Great Britain*. It resulted in the Public Health Act of 1848, when Government for the first time took responsibility for the health of its people. Chadwick was a prodigious worker, but his report had to draw on information from all over the country, the kind of information that we have seen in the reports on individual towns and villages. It also encompassed factories, prisons, Poor Law, emigration, and local government. The great spur was the rapid growth of population in the towns, with pressure on housing leading to back-to-back terraces and the installation of cellars in already overcrowded areas. It was abundantly clear that there was a correlation between overcrowding and disease.

Clean water supplies were crucial; today one litre of water costs five times as much in a Nairobi slum as in an American city, ten litres of water that flushes a loo in England provides the daily allocation for the washing, drinking and cooking needs of a person in the developing world. Water Aid also tells us that 6,000 children die each day from unsafe water and bad sanitation, 1.1 billion people (one sixth of the world's population) do not have access to safe water, and double that number do not have adequate sanitation. How many of the better-off realise that this is happening?

Bubonic plague had last struck in 1665. Some diseases suddenly appear, and eventually, for no apparent reason, disappear for a while. Although vaccination, discovered by Jenner, had brought smallpox under control for a while, once the disease waned people forgot about it – until it came back. We see in the Northumberland reports how prevalent it was. Cholera first struck in 1831-2, then in 1848-9, 1854, and 1867. Hundreds of thousands suffered and tens of thousands died. It really scared people because it struck down its victims so quickly. In the end, it went as quickly as it came, aided by better water supplies.

Typhus and consumption were more persistent and enduring. The sanitary report in Chadwick's document concentrates mainly on typhus – universally called 'fever' – both epidemic and endemic. It was there all the time, but came out in peak times. It was always lurking in narrow streets, closes and courtyards. As an epidemic it appeared from 1826-7, 1831-2, 1837, and 1846. Some noted that it appeared when trade was bad, when people had no work and little hope, and that its growth was related to living standards.

Not all the reports that we have seen mention consumption (or tuberculosis), but this was a greater killer than cholera or typhus. It was common but little understood, except there was a recognised link between the disease and under nourishment and squalor. Until the end of the nineteenth century it was an urban disease, and became the single most important cause of death after the 1830s.

Some reports, looking for some cause outside their own towns of disease, blamed incomers, especially the Irish, and the Irish Poor Inquiry of 1836 concluded that they 'are frequently the means of generating and communicating infectious disease'. So the incidence of typhus in 1846-7 was blamed by some on Irish migration at the time of the Famine. Others saw that it already flourished in overcrowded and insanitary areas.

To cope with crises, local Boards of Health sprang up, but would disband when epidemics waned. That something more permanent was needed was acknowledged in the Public Health Act; central control or direction had become essential.

Once the Northumberland towns had been visited by inspectors and recommendations made, we ask the question; did it make any difference? In many dramatic ways it did, especially in pinpointing the cause of disease and its spread, but we have today still not achieved ideal conditions. There was an outbreak of cholera in Hexham in 1853. Henry Woods, lodging in 'Holy Island', died. Three more cases followed: two were fatal. Cleansing took place in the form of hot lime and brushes. Streets were washed and swept, and home visits were arranged. More people died, and there were hundreds of cases of diarrhoea. A recommendation that pigsties should be removed was circulated.

One of the Board's medical officers was sent from London, and although he tried to be kind to the medical profession, he was critical that there was no regular system for getting rid of nuisances. He wrote:

> The town of Hexham is almost entirely unprovided with sewers. There is only one and scarcely any houses have connections with that. The ordure, filth of all sorts and ashes are collected in large pits and bins, and from the approaches to these being too narrow for a cart to enter, their contents are carried out to the street, and remain there till the carts pass to carry them away.

Much lime washing had been done, but the place was still filthy. He regarded many of the rooms that he visited as 'unwholesome and unfit for human habitation'. However, people in the town were strongly asking for change, though a vociferous group was still fighting against it. They lost, and in 1854 a Local Board of Health was appointed. The final death toll for cholera was twenty-three.

David Jennings' research into Hexham (Jennings, 1998) investigated two reports, one in 1872 and another in 1935, with the follow-up in mind. What follows is based upon that work. The General Board of Health was succeeded by the Local Board of Health, and then by the Urban District Council in 1894. To their reports can be added the results of census returns, for these particularly revolutionised the amount of information we have about who was living where, where they were born, and what their occupations were. The census of 1921 was the basis for a report by the Medical Officer of Health to the Urban District Council, which said that 1,721 people out of 8,843 had houses containing three or fewer rooms. That, of course, is a statistic and does not convey what people experienced as a result of overcrowding. Reports of 1872 and 1935 are very similar in their findings, so what had been done over sixty-five years? Was it a lack of money or a lack of interest, or both?

The *Report to the Urban Sanitary Authority* by John Hodgson in 1872 is certainly similar to the Rawlinson report of 1850. A description of a privy in the upper floor of Victoria Yard, Battle Hill, says that it was in a 'very foul condition', not fit for any person to use. It had no proper seat and was dangerous for children, with filthy matter lying around, oozing through the wall into the premises:

> This is the sole accommodation for about 70 people including the occupants of three lodging houses. The yard is strewed about with nauseous filth; there is no proper drainage and it is seldom swept. There is an ashpit but most of the refuse is thrown upon the open yard. I believe the lodging houses are not registered and are on this account illegal.

He recommends that the ashpits in the whole block should be done away with or reduced in size, and that water closets should replace privies. Mr Matthew Smith, who owned the property, was served notice. It turns out that he was a member of the Local Board of Health and its first chairman (from 1854-66)! In this case he complied, but his property at what is now Pudding Mews had to have another order served on it.

S.P.B. Mais (1935) wrote *England's Pleasance*, an account of a journey that began at Hexham – 'an admirable starting point because it contains outstanding examples of North-country beauty and North-country wretchedness'. When the driving force behind an unemployed men's club in Haugh Lane took him up Gilesgate to the then-modern post office he was handed three antiseptic lozenges before entering a dark narrow alley that led to a stone courtyard: 'A woman stood outside a doorway turning the handle of a mangle. Dirty water squeezed its way from the mangle over her feet and over the feet of several tiny children who coughed unhappily as they stood in the icy wind just looking at the stranger'. He climbed wooden stairs, and at the top of the fourth flight he thought he had been transported into a scene out of *Oliver Twist*. A woman showed him the bed where she, her husband and five children slept. They were trying to get out of this miserable room into a council house. There were three lavatories in the block for eighty people, and two didn't work. The houses had been condemned ten years ago, 'and yet I was in a stone's throw of the Abbey, and looking out over one of the greenest valleys in England'.

We know that the anecdote does not make a general rule, but we ask whether all the people in the town saw this picture. A letter in *The Hexham Courant* in 1930 from an indignant resident deplored the Medical Officers' reports that drew attention to anything unhealthy in the town. Why? 'There is no doubt whatever that Hexham has sustained considerable pecuniary loss solely attributable to these reports. And those ratepayers whose only means of making a living are entitled to protection and to receive every encouragement from elected councillors and paid officials'. Despite his protestations, there was no doubt that mortality figures from 1920 onwards were very high.

The east end and the building
of Hexham's new hospital.
(Matthew Hutchinson)

A survey by a group of local historians, including the author, of the Cockshaw area of Hexham, included recollections by people living in that area at the beginning of the last century. The figures quoted in slum clearance reports came to life with people's memories of living conditions in the 1920s and '30s. Many huge families lived in two or three rooms, with several families to a house. Communal street life was necessary, as there was no room in the houses. Lodging houses were still common. Several people described the dubious characters that lived in them. One Cockshaw resident spoke of her fear of passing the tenement called 'The Mystery'. She and her friends would pluck up courage to dash past the entrance. The census shows that a high proportion of people in lodging houses came from outside Hexham, particularly from Scotland and Ireland. Many people have described Cockshaw as one of Hexham's tough areas, where several notorious characters lived. Fights between the patrons of adjacent pubs 'The Tanner's Arms 'and 'The Skinners' Arms' seem to have been a regular Saturday-night feature of life there.

The bad smell of the burns was frequently mentioned. When the leather industry was operational, the water was described as being a thick yellow-brown sludge with a sickly smell that hung over everything. However, despite these problems, there was a great sense of community in the area. Many families were poor and prepared to share what they had. Extended families were common, with married children living close to their parents, providing security for the children. There were no latchkey children, as there was always a relative or friend to help out. Doors were rarely locked. Although the houses were crowded, land by the river at Tyne Green provided a back garden for them to play in.

All this is anecdotal, and one has to balance sometimes conflicting accounts based on individual experiences. This was the same area described in detail in Rawlinson's report. It came in for a slum clearance scheme; a large area of Gilesgate was declared 'an insanitary area' that required a radical scheme. In the Gilesgate ward the density of population was 11.1 per acre, compared with 1.7 in the Urban District, but the area with Holy Island at its centre had a density of 186 per acre. Disease was therefore much more prevalent there. They allowed forty-eight properties to remain, and demolished the rest in 1935 and 1936. As a result of these clearances and others in Hexham, large numbers of council houses were built at the east end between the two world wars to re-house the families. Beside them has now been built the large new Hexham General Hospital. It is only very recently that the attempt to tackle drainage problems of Cockshaw has resulted in expensive and far-reaching public works there.

Chapter 5

Education

Most people's education in the past was practical, so that they could cope with the problems of earning a living or just surviving. Skills were learnt on the job. However, there was a need for 'additional' education, especially when parents were keen for their children to 'get on'. This more formal learning had to be paid for. So the poor were not formally educated unless society demanded more skills or people with a conscience believed in more equality of opportunity.

The Priory trained novices, and we have an early record of such schooling when, in 1294, the Archbishop of York visited Hexham and appointed a new master. As we have seen, there is an account of how the Scots sacked the town, reportedly burning the boys alive in the school. There is no more information until we see references to 'The Old School' at the east end of the Priory church. After that, a continuous record of a Grammar School dates from its foundation in 1599 by a Charter from Queen Elizabeth – thus the name of the present Queen Elizabeth High School on a completely different site.

The Grammar School could have been in existence before its Charter. It was managed by twelve governors who lived in the parish, who feared God and were of a 'fair character'. The master had to say morning and evening prayers and ensure that all pupils went to evening prayers at the Abbey church on Saturdays and saints' days. They had weekly RE lessons, had to learn the catechism, and were questioned on the sermons that they heard. They were at school from 6 to 11 a.m. and 12.45 to 5 p.m. The curriculum included Latin and Greek; boys were required to speak Latin at school. Handwriting was taught, but not English language and literature. We do not know whether the curriculum was rigidly followed. Discipline was strict, and rules of conduct included forbidding them to go to alehouses. A sign of the times was that the statutes said that the pupils should not use weapons of any kind at or near the school, should not gamble or cheat their fellows, but that in all their doings they 'may glorify God to their master's credit'. They were, however, furnished with bows and arrows 'upon play days'.

In spite of its being called a 'Free School', Hexham boys had to pay yearly, and those from out of town had to pay considerably more. Much of the school's income came from interest on loans paid to local people. In 1677 the school reached the peak of its prosperity. Early in the next century the governors became very secretive about their accounts and management, and it seems that some embezzlement was going on.

The school, which may have been situated at the east end of the Abbey, was finally abandoned when a new school was built at Hallstile Bank in 1684, and this is something that we can actually see today. Sons of the local gentry and locals went there. The only recorded books were dictionaries. One hundred years later all was not well: in 1791 a letter from the governors to the Archbishop of York said that a properly qualified master was beyond their resources, and had been so for over fifty years, and that

The Old Grammar School next to the Old Gaol.

there had been complaints from parents. Demand outstripped supply; there were many boys ready for school who could be supported locally, but the system did not allow other schools to be established. What is very interesting about the complaints is the alleged character of the master, who was barbarous in his treatment of the boys and even used the school house as a pigsty. The income of the school fell, but eventually the school was repaired and a new master appointed who was so good at his job that the roll reached seventy-five to eighty pupils. He added maths and 'practical learning' to the Latin and Greek Grammar on the curriculum. With his resignation the governors could still not afford a master of arts to take over, so they had to change the constitution and brought in the Charity Commissioners from London to exercise some control over accounts and reports.

The governors in the second half of the nineteenth century were mainly townspeople, traders and professional men, and some of the local gentry. The curriculum became more 'modern' and fees were raised to pay for changes, but towards the end of the century the Free Grammar School wasn't good enough in numbers or income for the needs of the town. Crucially, in 1892 Northumberland County Council proposed a 'higher grade' school in Hexham; eventually this happened and the old school was put up for sale. The Education Act of 1902 made the County Council responsible for primary and secondary education, including technical education. A new school was built and opened in 1909 for children aged ten to eighteen with some boarders. There were classrooms for 240 children, equal numbers of boys and girls, a number reached by 1915. Overcrowding led to new classrooms being added. Grammar School education moved to the Hydro building in 1965.

Subscription Schools

As the Grammar School was the only 'endowed school' in Hexham, there were many little private schools and academies which people had to pay to attend. Churches and chapels had Sunday Schools,

Hexham Middle School, rear view, originally built as the Grammar School, which opened in 1910 with classrooms for 120 boys and 120 girls.

allowing about 500 children to receive some education in 1829. There was concern about the lack of education of children of the poor; this was thought to be bad for national and local welfare, missing a chance to teach them morality and religion. A group formed a school in 1813 at the head of the Skinners' Burn (Eastgate area) to take 240 children. Scholars paid 1d a week, except Poor House children. Its quality depended on the competence of its master, and in 1852 we hear of a curriculum that included oral work instead of a rote system in the 3Rs, with geography, history and Bible instruction included. At this time boys and girls were kept separate. Soon a new building was needed; work began in 1855 and the school was finished in 1856, in two blocks with windows and a fireplace. Again there was a need to expand to include more children, and in 1873 the Hexham School Board was founded.

The Sele School was expanded to take 900 children; the County Council took it over in 1903 with the Board Schools, and a new school was built. Churches continued to have their own schools, such as St Mary's, and in general private schools decreased as public schools increased. This is only a sketch of the growth and development of education in Hexham, and its story is reflected in many other parts of Northumberland. Today Hexham has a High School, two Middle Schools (for children aged nine to thirteen), three First Schools, nursery school provision and classes for adults. At the time of writing there is a division of opinion about whether the Three-Tier system of High, Middle and First schools should be replaced by a Two-Tier system. In favour of retaining the status quo, but not in any way excluding its reform, is the fact that local schools all do well and that the needs of one of the largest rural areas in Britain favours smaller schools closer to home. The contrary argument is that larger units are more efficient and provide more opportunities for varied learning.

Whatever the outcome, the present location of schools reflects the history of education in Hexham to some extent, with earlier survivals still present. Architecture and documents add to our knowledge of this process. These schools are: The Sele School, Hexham East and St Mary's First Schools; Hexham Middle School and St Joseph's Middle School; and Queen Elizabeth High School. There are two special schools in the area: the Priory School in Hexham, and Dilston College, just outside.

Chapter 6

Communications

Today Hexham is very fortunate to have an east-west railway from Newcastle to Carlisle and a link to a major road, although like every other town in Britain it has some serious traffic problems because of its system of old roadways, parking, and occasional problems caused by public utility works like the recent essential relaying of new water mains. The number of people relying on a car for private transport, especially the incomprehensibly large car and waste of fuel, continues to add problems.

Historically, roads in and around Hexham have always been bad since the departure of the Roman legions. Hadrian's Wall to the north of the town and the earlier Roman frontier had its own essential, well-established communications, including splendid bridges across the River Tyne at Corbridge and Chesters, but after that the river remained an obstacle except when its waters were low enough for horses and carts to cross by fording places. Some of the stones from the bridge at Coria were later built into the crypt at Hexham, so presumably by the seventh century it was already sufficiently decayed to use it as building material.

It is not possible to compile a continuous record of roads in the area. Many people could cross the land if they knew it well, and armies and smaller warring bands did so, but one could hardly say that there were good roads. Take the seventeenth century, for example. Three military men on a seven-week journey from Norwich in 1634 reported their difficulties reaching Hexham. Just when they had coped with many dangers they faced a great gulf, the River Tyne, where there was neither bridge nor boat, and just managed to cross the ford with their horses with the help of a guide. Having reached the town, they found it small, with poor inhabitants and a decayed 'cathedral-like church', but with a 'fair and handsome' house where the Lord of the Manor, Sir John Fenwick, lived. He gave them free entertainment.

In 1639-40 the defences of Hexham were inspected, and the town was not thought worth fortifying. The river was fordable, but it was a place 'where no carriages can come and go to the Borders'. The report concluded that 150 musketeers could defend the two towers as 'one cannot march that way without great difficulty, and ordnance I would not trust in them'. A circuit judge in 1676 commented on, 'the hideous road along the Tine, so bad that he had to abandon a carriage in favour of a horse'. Having got there, he found Hexham an ugly town with 'nothing worthy of notice'. The Shire he considered obnoxious, with thieves living in 'shieles' (temporary cottages). In 1698 Celia Fiennes was more impressed with the town, with the two gates leading into it, broad streets and a Market Place with 'a Town Hall on the Market Crosse'.

The Jacobite Risings (1715-45) dominated much of the early eighteenth century, and the movement of armies was hampered by road conditions. Imagine the problems of moving provisions and guns from east to west, for example, and one understands why the road that made use of tonnes of Roman stone taken from the Wall and its forts was constructed north of Hexham. Today you may drive on a road that actually lies above the foundations of that Wall with a ditch on one side and its vallum on the other. Good roads are essential to the movement of armies, as the Romans well knew, and as later armies were to realise. When the first Jacobite Rising took place, it was led locally by the Earl of Derwentwater (Dilston) and his strong Catholic following. The Pretender (James III) was proclaimed as the rightful king in the Market Place in Hexham, although some people like Sir William Blackett 'managed to keep out of the way'. This was not surprising as he was a Member of Parliament and owned several local lead mines. The rebels stayed in Hexham for three days, stealing arms and horses, and then moved off to their fate. There were still local Jacobites in 1745, and the rebels concentrated on the west of England. General Wade, the eventual victor over the rebels, stayed briefly in Hexham on his way towards Carlisle with the English army, but the roads were so bad that he returned to Newcastle.

It is salutary to remember that until 1746 the only communication between Newcastle and Carlisle was a bridleway, and that packhorses were the only means of transporting goods. The 1745 rebellion exposed the problem, for Charles Stuart's army was able to reach Derby before enough troops could be mobilised against him. The Military Road was built, and then it was supplemented by a mail coach road through Hexham and Haltwhistle. It took three days for carts to travel from Newcastle to Carlisle.

In the following century, things began to improve with the introduction of turnpike roads, with tollgates to help pay for them, and with the building of bridges. However, before that there were some disasters. In 1770 Sir Walter Blackett, Lord of the Manor, financed the first modern Tyne Bridge, but the following year there was a disastrous flood that affected all Northumberland rivers. Although the bridge at Corbridge survived, Hexham's was destroyed in a flood that caused extensive damage yet affected only a few people, who requested compensation.

The next bridge, Smeaton's, collapsed in a blizzard in 1780 – the year following its construction. There was much better luck with the next bridge, built on the same site but with better foundations, and this is the one that crosses into Hexham today.

As the prosperity of Hexham depended on its link with the farming areas, good roads were and are essential, not only into the town but within it. The turnpike roads, such as that linking farms between Hexham and the grain port of Alnmouth (The Alemouth, or Corn Road) were essential to expansion of trade, but one proposal in 1825 to build a turnpike road over the Sele aroused such anger within the town because it was considered to belong to the people for their leisure that it was eventually thrown out by Mrs Beaumont, wife of the Lord of the Manor, Colonel Beaumont, who stated that 'no power upon earth shall induce Colonel Beaumont and myself to do any thing to deprive the inhabitants of Hexham, of the comforts and privileges they have so long enjoyed in the Seal'. Good for her, but this emphatic statement had been preceded by protests, many in verse, in broadsheets. An encouraging aspect of Hexham's history is the way in which landowners have donated land and facilities to the townspeople, so that today the Sele and its surroundings and the Abbey Grounds remain splendid assets. A peal of bells greeted the news, and the road that took precedence, 'The Temperley Line', was established, still leading out of town past the modern cemetery on the way to join the A69.

There had to be a way of creating and maintaining good roads and a system grew up piecemeal: interested parties could put forward a Bill to Parliament. From 1751-1772, more and more applications were made. The Newcastle-Carlisle Military Road began in 1751, paid for with Government money but operated as a turnpike. The Corn Road from Hexham was turnpiked in 1752, a necessary step as the demand for more corn intensified. This coincided with the enclosure of more land for arable usage, a reversal of the policy that had put sheep pasture at a priority, often at the expense of closing villages. By the mid-eighteenth century, large areas were enclosed with new walls and hedges, and arable farming was intensified to feed the rapidly-growing population. Remaining fields were enclosed, and commons and wasteland were cultivated. The more powerful the landlord, the easier this was – and it was done by an Act of Parliament. We can trace the process on maps. The pattern of rectangular fields with hedges and walls was reflected in the roads, with straight lines and sharp corners at the plough headlands. Look along the route of the Corn Road and see the considerable amount of rig and furrow fields, not of the medieval pattern of wide, S-shaped curves, but of straighter, narrower lines. Follow the road from Hexham to the grain port of Alnmouth, and the contrast between straight, 'modern' sections and the older curves and corners is apparent.

Coach travel increased on the new roads; in Britain turnpikes covered one fifth of total public highways, with parishes still mainly responsible for them. Wheeled traffic replaced packhorses and speeded up travel considerably; competition among carriers kept prices down. The early nineteenth century changed the way roads were constructed; it was the age of Telford and McAdam, when there was a graded build-up of road surfaces, the straightening of sections and a reduction of gradients.

A great moment in Northumberland's history was the beginning of the railway age. It is extraordinary to see so much evidence of an extensive railway network and to realise how far-reaching this form of transport became. The amount of effort that went into building railways was phenomenal, seeming almost compulsive. The whole business had to be preceded by careful planning of routeways and costs, landowners had to be convinced or bought off, shareholders convinced, and the labour brought in to do the job had to be housed and paid for. The risks were in human lives and financial outlay. The conviction that steam was the future was absolute, the industrial base and expertise to make it happen was firm in the North East, and rail took precedence over roads. Northumberland is left with this legacy, largely in the form of overgrown flat beds where lines used to run, bridges in various states of decay, and, near the Tyne at Hexham, we see the remains of the pillars that carried bridges over the river to the north. Many of the well-built stations, houses and depots have become private homes or are put to other uses. Hexham, however, is very fortunate in that it retains one of the oldest working lines in the world. Today the station is diminished, with some unused platforms and outbuildings, including a water tower, but the Victorian ironwork so characteristic of Victorian architecture is still there and the two platforms on the east-west route are still used.

The story has been well told in many publications, but the forerunner of its history was written by Tomlinson in his *North Eastern Railway*, edited in 1967 by Ken Hoole. It is a microcosm of the visions, planning and frustrations of the Railway Age, and a tale worth retelling – at least in part. The railway, designed to link sea to sea, was a very exciting concept, but not the only one, for an extensive canal system was also proposed. A straightforward plan was devised that involved the removal of only one cottage along its route, not interfering very much with landowners' property, and involving the use of horse-drawn carriages! This would have been quieter than and not as objectionable as some steam locomotives.

On 12 November 1825 the first parliamentary notice was given of the main line and seven branch lines. George Stephenson was appointed by Greenwich Hospital to survey the land on the north side of the Tyne, beginning at Warden Bridge near Hexham, to the east to Corbridge, then to Thornborough, Heddon, and Town Moor, Newcastle. By 1826 proposals were not ready to put to Parliament, so they did not apply that session. In 1828 a line was definitely fixed. Thirty-five landowners objected. Charles Bacon of Styford and his son Charles Bacon Gray were the biggest thorn in the flesh – no matter what the planners did to accommodate them, they objected, and on no condition would they allow a railway to go though their property. Others saw that this blocking tactic would not be their advantage. The position was that there was only one vehicle between Carlisle and Newcastle to carry Newcastle papers and the occasional passenger, two carriers and two stagecoaches which took eight and a half hours to cover the

Hexham railway station.
(Birtley Aris)

distance. The road was crowded at times and it took three days for other forms of transport. The success of the Stockton-Darlington railway was there for all to see: it was cheap and rapid. The other landlords put pressure on the objectors, although Mr Bacon Gray tried to convince Parliament that his objections were that the best route had not been selected. After a fight in Parliament he gave way, eventually picking up the hefty sum of £3,000 in compensation, and the royal assent was given to the Bill on 22 May 1829. Thus we had the largest railway sanctioned by Parliament at that time.

In its original form this was very different from what it was to become, for the Bill stated: 'No locomotive or moveable steam engine shall be used on the said railways or tramroads for drawing wagons or other carriages, or for any other purpose whatsoever'. When the concept of traction changed, some landowners were protected from being in sight of any steam engines from their houses, including Charles Bacon of Styford and Nicholas Leadbitter of Warden. The rail was intended for public use, on the payment of a toll, and a list of goods and prices was laid down.

The company brought in an engineer (Francis Giles) from London to check the route again and report on it; he approved. A very large board of directors was then appointed, and work began in March 1830 at the west between Blenkinsopp and Carlisle whilst there was still a problem about what to do at the east end. Meanwhile, a terminus was fixed at Blaydon. Economy was an important consideration for these early lines, and in contrast to the superb architecture of so many stations on the later line from Alnwick to Cornhill, on some stations there was no platform. On the Newcastle-Carlisle railway some had a platform on one side only. There were some good stations, of which the large permanent station at Hexham remains an example. Until 1844 the Stocksfield-Hexham line was only a single track; at the Farnley tunnel near Corbridge the single line was doubled.

From this distance, contemporary accounts give us so much about the wrangles over routes, about the protection of property, of the sheer effort and expertise – legal, scientific and financial – that went into such enterprises that it appears like a huge bubbling cauldron from which the product may emerge pure or marred. Shareholders expected to make a fortune, and the incompetence of those entrusted with their money could mean ruin. Debates raged in localities through to Parliament. Egos were enhanced and destroyed. What is often neglected is information about the workforce of 'navvies', which was the only means by which the building work could all happen once decisions about money and routes had been sorted out.

This railway succeeded. On 28 June 1836, the 7.5 mile stretch from Hexham to Haydon Bridge

An early engraving of Hexham
railway station, with the principal
town buildings on the hill behind.
Today, only the main Newcastle-
Carlisle line is in operation.

opened. A procession of two trains started from Blaydon, pulled by engines called *Hercules* and *Sampson*. One carriage was occupied by the Allendale band. On 26 July the Hartleyburn and Brampton railway opened as a private colliery line to replace an older waggonway.

The opening of the west portion of the main line was a grand affair watched by 40,000 people when a procession of four trains carrying about 400 passengers ran between Newcastle and Greenhead. Somehow the story of official openings has become something like a comedy script, not always funny for those involved. On this occasion the train carrying the mayor and corporation became detached when a coupling gave way. The others had to wait for it for three quarters of an hour.

That was nothing compared with the opening of the whole stretch of sixty-one miles on 18 June 1836 (Waterloo Day), when five trains set off from Newcastle for Carlisle. It is best to let the historian of the railways, Tomlinson, tell us the story.

> The Corporation of Carlisle and the directors from the west crossed the river in the barges of the Mayor of Newcastle and the Trinity House, the other visitors in steam packets. This part of the day's proceedings was marred by a regrettable incident. A gangway between the Quay and one of the steam packets gave way and twelve or thirteen of the passengers from the second train, among whom were two ladies in dainty silk dresses, a physician and two surgeons from Carlisle got a ducking in the river, which, fortunately, was not more than three or four feet deep at the time.

From the Close, the civic bodies of Newcastle and Carlisle marched in procession by way of Grey Street to the Assembly Rooms, where they breakfasted with the directors. On returning to Redheugh about an hour after the advertised time for starting, they found the carriages occupied. The corporation of Gateshead, by arriving in good time, had secured their seats, but the rest of the reserved carriages had been invaded by the crowd. 'Thus situated', to quote *The Gateshead Observer*, 'the civic authorities were reduced to the necessity of looking for seats, and the chief magistrates of Carlisle and Newcastle were obliged to look for refuge in a pig-cart'.

The eating of food and the drinking of toasts figures largely in rail ceremonies, which led to over-indulgence, and a lack of punctuality! Anyway, one can imagine the affront to dignity among some officials, but this was to be shared by all.

The procession set off, and fog gave way to rain at Ryton and continued all the way to Brampton. Three thousand five hundred people took part, including the historian John Hodgson, who wrote a little gem for us in a letter to his wife on 19 June after the event:

I may add that one side of my bag, by lying under the seat on which I had sat, had, for an hour or more, before I remembered it, amused itself with talent as a sponge and drunk up so much of the water that poured from our roof of umbrellas as to make my night things wet as itself and as dirty as the sheep truck on which we were carried: for you must know that its office was new yesterday: sheep and oxen from it on their way to Newcastle had been in the habit of grazing on the beauties of the Tyne: but now it became a pen of bipeds not hairy enough to cover themselves at once with a sealing by which each defended his own head but powered a precious stream into the cap or down the shoulders of his neighbour!

Thomas Sopwith's dairy recorded that it took three hours and forty-three minutes to get from Blaydon to Carlisle, of which only two hours thirty-seven minutes were spent travelling. The stops were at Stocksfield, Corbridge, Hexham, Haydon Bridge, Haltwhistle and Milton. The last of the procession of trains arrived at Carlisle an hour after it was timed to leave. The passengers had been cooped up for a long time, so naturally when they arrived at Carlisle, 'A disorderly stampede for refreshments took the place of a procession into the town which was to have formed part of the day's proceedings'. When it was nearing the time to leave, 'early comers took possession of the covered carriages, entering the windows when the doors were locked. Several ladies of portly town councillors, with a temporary loss of dignity, secured comfortable seats in this way'.

Time had to be allowed for the trains to be prepared for the return journey, so when the trains were supposed to arrive at Redheugh they were still in Carlisle. 'Passengers who had taken their seats at 6.30 p.m. did not get away until nearly ten o'clock, having had to remain for over three hours exposed to the drenching showers in a comfortless station' – presumably with no refreshments and no loos. The ladies had dressed for a summer's day.

But that wasn't the end: one train collided with the back of another. 'Some carriages and a tender were thrown off the line and two passengers injured, one having a rib broken and the other a hip dislocated'. So everyone had to sit miles from anywhere surrounded by wild country until 1 a.m., to the great anxiety of those waiting at Redheugh for their return. 'Thousands of people waited all night'. The first train arrived at 3 a.m. and the last at 6 a.m.

These events established the Newcastle-Carlisle railway: it meant that by 1834 lead was being carried from Hexham to Blaydon by rail for refining, and that in 1835 passengers could travel by steam locomotive. This did away with the stagecoaches which used the turnpike roads, and more lines branched out to support the lead and coal industries. The railways could also carry leather products and fresh vegetables to Tyne valley towns. The railway industry itself used a great deal of leather in its upholstery. Better travel meant also that more people could come into the town, either to work or for a holiday. The consequence of increased commercial activity was a rise in population (3,427 in 1801 to 7,071 by 1900) and an extensive building programme which, although at first adding to the historic town centre, began to spread outwards. A survey, however cursory, of Hexham buildings shows clearly this expansion.

The railways brought tourism. In 1851 'H.U.S.' of Newcastle published a *Handbook to the Newcastle and Carlisle Railway*, intended as a guidebook for the traveller, and it included the Roman Wall. For the man of business, it included the principal towns and 'commodious inns etc.' Hexham is included prominently as a town of 4,742 people. He writes:

Hexham station today.

Though the trade has materially declined of late years, a considerable business is yet carried out in tanned
leather, hats and gloves, and the early gardens supply Newcastle and the neighbourhood, largely with finest
fruits and vegetables. The market place is a good sized area, with a row of covered shambles.

He gives a brief history of the town with a fairly detailed description of the Abbey. He mentions the
several 'dissenting Chapels', and commends the 'Seal' as 'an open space of ground, at the west end of
the town', which 'affords a delightful promenade to the inhabitants, and commands an extensive and
varied prospect over a fine range of country. From the salubrity of the air, and general beauty of the
surrounding district, Hexham is indeed a most desirable place of residence'.

He tells of the Battle of Hexham Levels, of Queen Margaret and her son's meeting with the outlaws
in the wood, and of the Hexham Riot of 1761. He also mentions the 'Hermitage, the residence of
Stamp Brookshank Esq.... and ancient chapel and chantry, founded by the monks of Hexham during
the tenth century, and occupied by them till the Dissolution in 1535'. For the traveller he notes that
'Hexham contains many excellent Inns, the principal of which are the White Hart and Black Bull, both
comfortable and commodious houses. For the convenience of passengers, omnibuses ply to and from
the town, to meet the Railway trains'.

This is a good example not only of tourist hard sell for the town, but underlines that the railways had many
uses. Agricultural traffic was always important to the railway, particularly for cattle and sheep. Hexham and
Bellingham held important agricultural shows, when there was a great demand for transport. There was also
a warning of the danger of disease spreading, for when in 1866 there was an outbreak of 'cattle plague' there
was a proposal to stop railway traffic, but it was heavily defeated. However, it was agreed that the railway
companies should order their staff 'to disinfect and cleanse out all their trucks at Newcastle'.

Today, although there is frequent concern about overcrowded roads, we have been stupid enough as
a nation not to consider the revival of an efficient railway system. Privatisation was not the panacea it
was promised to be. There are constant scares about reducing services on the Carlisle-Newcastle line.
Like it or not, people are adamant that they have every right to occupy one large car for themselves; this
is something which must be challenged now that the very sources of our energy are threatened.

Hexham station, reached in 1833, was one of those designed rather like a country cottage; a drawing
of 1835 shows it as a gabled house with a porch, when passenger traffic began to Blaydon; it was
later altered. It was lighted on the east by Tudor-style windows and a bay. The north had the main

porticoed entrance. The ground floor had a kitchen, living room and public room. The first floor had two bedrooms reached by stairs. This was at a time when there was an emphasis on economy in station building on the early lines; at some stations there wasn't a platform, and on the Newcastle-Carlisle line some stations had a platform on only one side. Hexham was a station that seemed built to last from the outset. Once it had a roofed train shed, replaced by platform awnings, and the footbridge had a cover. There were facilities for the Allendale branch stations at the west end, with a bay for the local trains to Newcastle at the east. There was a goods yard and engine shed on the south of the line.

Hexham was not only important for the town, but as a junction for other systems. The North British Hawick and Riccarton Junction was about a mile west of Hexham. The NER line to Allendale joined the Carlisle line at the same junction; this closed to passengers in 1930 and to goods in 1950. This line never looked likely to be profitable; originally it was built in stages from 1866-68 for use in the lead industry, but this was in decline. It actually ended at Catton (renamed as Allendale station in 1898) because money and commitment ran out. While it operated, it carried livestock, timber, coal, fodder and general merchandise as well as passengers. What we see now at Hexham is the survival of the earliest east-west railway, but the branches have gone and the continued use of the line must not be taken for granted. However, it would be folly to do anything other than improve the service.

Obviously Hexham did not develop with any idea of the pressure that individual car ownership would bring. Each time any development in building is proposed within the town voices are raised about 'access' and further congestion. People who buy terraced houses with no private parking facilities have to park in front of their houses, with no secure legal right to do so. Others park there, even groups who share cars and drive one to Newcastle, and some who work in Hexham from outside take up spaces too. Selfishness plays a great part in all this. Today, Tesco has free parking for three hours, whether people shop there or not. The Co-op is very tolerant of parking, even though not many shop there today. Other spaces have to be paid for, and bring in a reasonable income for the council. If parking were not restricted in the town centre, the greediest would monopolise it. No matter how many traffic surveys are made (at the expense of the council tax payers) there has been no clear long-term solution proposed. Hexham is not alone in facing an insoluble problem.

When buses became popular, there was a real problem in the town. Beaumont Street was earmarked by the companies as a bus parking place in 1928, and there was an outcry from the townspeople, reported in *The Hexham Courant*. Attention was drawn to the fact that the Abbey Grounds had been partly purchased by public money, which also maintained them and the street. They wanted to maintain the quiet of the street where people could contemplate beauty and the war memorial:

> Bus traffic on Sunday evening is disturbing to the churches in the street... the congestion of the traffic in the evenings, especially on Saturdays and Sundays, is such as to deprive the ordinary pedestrian of the proper use of the footpath on the west side of the street, and has become a serious danger..

The objectors were not against bus traffic, which they regarded as 'one of the conveniences of life', but were against subsidising private transport for people who paid no rates.

> It is felt that the present proposal is virtually an attempt to establish at public expense a 'bus station for privately-owned buses, with all the obstruction, congestion, smells, dirt, grease and litter necessarily associated with such a use in the most handsome street in town.

The problem of finding a suitable central place for a bus park remains a problem today, though at the end of 2006 there are some signs that there may be a solution.

Chapter 7

Some Buildings

The Workhouse

An interesting way of coming to grips with the history of Hexham, as already indicated, is to examine its buildings carefully for what they tell us of their use and history.

Outside the town centre there many interesting and attractive domestic developments that have spread out, mainly on agricultural land to the east and west. Thus Leazes Lane and Leazes Crescent in the west end are actually named after fields. There are many rows of good-quality terraces, built of stone and brick in the late nineteenth and early twentieth centuries, with some outstanding large buildings built by prosperous local business men, mainly in the nineteenth century. Some have changed their function since they were built. Others have disappeared. For example, the War Memorial Hospital, built by public subscription just off Eastgate, was demolished recently for a new estate. Some large buildings have become care homes. Since the nineteenth century there have been two major developments: one is the spread of quality housing up the southern slopes of Hexham towards the ridge that overlooks the Tyne valley, and along the road leading west out of Hexham, and the other is the planned council estates, outside the town centre. Altogether there is a great variety of building styles, materials and period. Every time land becomes available, it is built on, as Hexham has become one of the most desirable places to live in England.

Many former derelict industrial buildings and sites have been reused for housing and offices. Within the town itself is an interesting variety of building styles of many periods, some of which we have already seen. The emphasis of this book has had to be on the historic town centre, but I have chosen three out-of-centre sites to show other aspects of the town's history.

The Workhouse lies on the Corbridge road opposite the modern hospital. In popular fiction, the workhouse is a Victorian institution, Dickensian in its gloom, where the destitute were housed, fed and given some sort of work. Husbands were separated from wives and families split (as in *Christmas Day in the Workhouse*). It was one way in which local authorities, directed from London, came to terms with the problems of poverty and vagrancy, the responsibility for funding being placed on the rates.

In Hexham, the Workhouse was the Poor Law Institution which later became a hospital, then a nurses' home. Built in 1839 with its classically-proportioned windows, it had a Jacobean-type centre and cupola added in 1883. What else do we know about it? Information about the workhouse is kept by the Northumberland Records Office, and there are reports in the local paper. These show that the rules governing the Workhouse became very much the concern of central government, and they dictated standards that they expected to be kept, but that the Board of Guardians took their responsibilities seriously, even under the pressure of dealing with some difficult cases.

The Workhouse – the
master's house.

The buildings have had changes of use and many attachments have been made to the original. A building is so much material, but documents may put some life into them by recounting what went on there. Just three examples in the early twentieth century will serve to give examples, each in its way very revealing.

In 1904 the Guardians' minute book reports that Margaret Hall was ordered to the Workhouse with her four children. Her husband had left them destitute and the police could not trace him. It was important to the authorities to catch such wayward parents who left their families to be cared for by local rates. She too left the children at the Workhouse, and was not to be found either! The case was reported in *The Hexham Courant*, and the minutes and the newspaper published a letter from the mother to the matron, which is quite remarkable. It is not couched in the language one might expect from a deserter:

The Union Workhouse, Hexham, October 12, 1907.

My dear matron, I have often thought of doing this, and at last I find sufficient courage to do so. I am leaving you to try to find a house for my children. I am leaving the children for a while, as to take them out and begin on nothing would mean them worse off than they are at present. The separation will be hard to bear on both sides, but I trust it will be for their own good in the end. Be kind to them and tell them that I shall come and take them out to a home of their own. Dolly and Tot are sure to fret at first, but tell them that their mother will always be thinking of them and hopes they will be good. Now dear matron, I thank you for all your kindness to me during the time I have been with you. Trusting you will forgive me for what I have done, and hoping it will be for the best. I am sincerely yours, Margaret Hall.

In order to cope with the problem of unwanted children, Hexham had a Boarding-Out Committee which tried to place children in private homes for payment. In this case, one of the children, the eldest boy, was a particular problem. In 1913 his foster parent said that, 'I really can do with him no longer and the language he has uttered to me lately is most serious'. The committee considered sending him to Canada. His brother and two sisters were boarded out, but there were the problems of payment to foster parents and of the children to deal with. Eventually, at the age of fourteen, the elder boy was employed on a farm at Carrshield; what is interesting is that the Guardians did not just give him up after they were no longer responsible financially for him, but asked that someone should keep an eye on him until he was eighteen.

A second example is of a German who had been living with his wife and seven children, all born in England, at Blyth when war broke out with Germany. The father was interned on the Isle of Man. His wife and children came to Hexham in 1915; she died in 1917, and the children were left destitute, so the Guardians took on the care of the children in the Workhouse after they had been found living in conditions that 'were hardly fit for human habitation'. The father was allowed to visit Hexham for the funeral, and he wanted the children to go to a Roman Catholic House at Tudhoe and Gainford. His wife had applied for their admission before she died. Eventually the children went with the Workhouse master to Darlington, to be housed in Roman Catholic homes.

The third instance is of a very different nature. A boat arriving at Newcastle brought an Asian sailor who ended up in Hexham by walking there. He could not understand the local speech, and was found wandering around the town. The Guardians became involved as he had no means of support. The man was able to indicate that he had decided to take a walk from his ship in Newcastle and had ended up in Hexham. The Guardians, after trying to get him back to his ship, sought financial help from the Foreign and Colonial Office. Their help was to give directions to a 'Hostel for Asians' in London.

The seaman was sent by train, with a note pinned to his clothes, to the home, only to turn up again in Hexham. He said he did not like the hostel and did like Hexham. He was finally disposed of when he was put on a ship they had found for him out of Middlesbrough.

As we have seen elsewhere in this book, the nineteenth century was one in which central government intervened more and more in local government. In the case of the Workhouse, there were strict regulations in force. For example, when a plan was put forward to extend the Workhouse buildings, the plans were returned with corrections; they would not allow an extension to be built end-on, but quoted regulations which insisted that the new building should be built parallel, with space between for air and light.

The Hydro

The Hydro is now is part of Queen Elizabeth High School, occupying a high site on the edge of town. It was built as the Tynedale Hydropathic Establishment as a spa and hotel. It was the brainchild of John Hope Jnr, who ran a successful tea and grocery warehouse, and a small candle factory. He also supplied cattle feed, fertilizer and seeds to farmers. His attention turned to the property market in the 1870s. He bought property called Westfield House at public auction and set about raising capital to transform it into the Hydropathic Establishment. The house was left, more or less intact, with corresponding Italianate additions. The company chairman claimed that the venture was not only to raise money, but 'it is my duty to do all I can to stem the tide of intemperance'. The local paper carried this advertisement when it opened:

> This establishment is now open for the reception of visitors. It has accommodation for over 100, and will be found replete with every comfort and convenience. Two bedrooms are believed to be the largest and best furnished of the kind in the kingdom. The situation is most salubrious, and the view, commanding some 20 miles of the valley of the Tyne, one of the finest in the North of England. Terms: £2 12s 6d a week.

The Hydro today, from the rear, part of the High School.

The opening was on 7 August 1879; the railway station was very busy and the Abbey bells rang out a welcome. Rest, recreation and temperance were the objectives. Nearly 300 attended the grand opening and feasted and danced for an afternoon and evening. Very sadly, the instigator of all this, John Hope, had fallen into debt at a time of general depression, and no one came forward to help him. He lost his house and everything else he owned, went to Newcastle, never came back, and died in 1909.

That was not the end of the venture. Stanley Gallagher, a successful Newcastle quayside businessman, linked by marriage to the Maling family, stepped in first as chairman of the management company then as owner. A descendant, Christopher Bradley, describes his recollections of the Hydro in *The Hexham Historian* (No. 11), when the hotel had its own vegetable gardens, greenhouses, and animals. The hotel bought a small bus to link with the trains. He says that 'the hotel served a fine menu, prepared by an army of chefs with tall hats'.

When you entered the hotel at the front there was a smell of cigars and expensive perfumes. The hotel was described as a hydropathic health centre, where one could have steam baths or take the water from the little fountain in the winter gardens fed from an underground spring, with foul smelling water, which was supposed to be therapeutic. The Turkish baths department had massage tables, and wooden boxes in the shape of arm chairs, with two doors at the front and a hole at the top for the bather's head. Once inside steam was released and the patient had the excess fat and impurities sweated out. This would be followed by diving into a cold water plunge, a small swimming pool with decorative tiles.

The remains of the House of Correction on Tyne Green.

This is from first-hand experience of his life there as a boy, and how refreshing it is to have such an account. He saw several wedding receptions 'attended by celebrities with large cars'. In 1931 his grandfather caught a cold, followed by pneumonia and died. Christopher Bradley had spent his formative years from five to fourteen at the Hydro, but had to leave his house on Beech Hill, 'and life was never the same again'.

The Hydro offered facilities to local people as well as to visitors, such as the baths there. It was very popular for its tea and dinner dances. In 1941 it became a children's sanatorium, then in 1950 it became part of the Northern Counties College of Domestic Science, then a teacher training college. It became part of the High School in 1974. Today one part used for public concerts is the Winter Gardens, a large conservatory added in 1907.

In *The Hexham Courant* there is a lengthy account by 'J.D.' of a holiday he spent at the Hydro for Christmas and the New Year. Again, the personal touch is what makes the history of a building so interesting. He had spent every Christmas there since it came into the hands of 'the present company' and was delighted that every manager, male or female, had added to the comfort of the guests, none more so than the present one. His complaint was that there was too much food to choose from, and he gives examples of exotic meals served there.

On Christmas Day the boys from the Abbey Choir sang for nearly 150 guests. The ballroom was decorated profusely, the Clemil band, a Hexham group, played and young and old danced. There were bridge parties in the spacious lounge, and 'the smokeroom had its contingent of more staid mankind'. The next day, Boxing Day, brought rain and snow, and the hills to the south were pure white. The sun came out when lunch was over, and the 'Britishness' of the concourse was shown in the way 'they settled down to make the best of it', with 'reading, writing, ping-pong'. The same evening there was a power failure in the Tyne valley, and candles were brought out:

What a dinner that was by candlelight. What a promenade of fancy costumes....Nay, one dear young thing was heard to declare, in answer to a remark of a chum, 'Oh, but I rather like it, you know; it's such good fun hunting the fellows out of dark corners'... One did feel a bit sorry for individual wearers of historic or foreign costumes, because a man that might have been a matador looked like a coal-bearer, and equally so a lady whose dress was very closely scanned had the elements of classic good taste, yet by the light of the 'mould' would have passed muster as a scullery maid.

Two hundred people watched the parade. On the next day there was a dinner followed by 'a really tip-top orchestral concert', with violin and xylophone solos. Then two ladies did some humorous sketches. The next day brought a fire that began and ended in the furnace supplying the radiators in the Winter Garden, the corridors and the lounge.

As a spectacle it was a failure, but as evidence of existence by means of a suffocating smoke, it was more than perfect. Every door, many windows and each ventilator was used for getting rid of the obnoxious element...

Thus the days passed. Dancing and revels, a treasure hunt, dancing of the pupils of Miss Lazenby, not an hour of all the eight or nine days dull or void of interest. Finally, following upon an extra good dinner, and we had thought already that the Chef had excelled himself, even to the extent of having a braw Highland laddie to play in the 'Haggis', which became an entrée. If the piper looked proud, no less so was the chef, as, followed by one of his kitchen help-meets, he pranced behind the man in kilts, bearing aloft a huge dish of the compound which has evoked paeans and poems of praise all down the ages. The sight was inspiring even if the digestion was not improved by partaking of the savoury. Thence to the ballroom, where for some hours King Carnival reigned supreme. Later to the corridors all must go, for the curtain was to be rung down upon 1930.

Little did he know that two years later Hitler was to come to power in Germany.

The House of Correction

The House of Correction, already referred to, stands out in complete contrast to this pleasure house. It was opened in 1784 for the imprisonment of petty criminals, and closed in 1871.

For over seventy years magistrates had asked for such a place, as Hexham attracted so many beggars and vagrants. John Dayleas was appointed as its first keeper. The building, originally a rented private house, was then purchased by the magistrates in 1794. It was extended in the 1820s. There is a plan which shows that it fronted Chareway, with a public road on one side and the Governor's garden on the other. In between, the prisoners had a day-room on the ground floor and the governor had his kitchen and a room with a lodging above it. The prisoners' rooms were above these. Servants were housed there, and the prisoners' work-room. Behind were yards for the governor and prisoners.

The house was sold in 1860 and all that remains today is the prisoners' day-room and sleeping cells above it. The windows are barbed slits. The cells still have heavy iron doors and shackles.

Kristensen and Dallison (2006) have a plan of the building and a photograph of cottages that were converted from the governor's residence. These were demolished in 1972 and yet they were listed buildings. Now there is a bus depot/garage on the site.

Chapter 8

Churches Together and Apart

Although there has been a significant unification of churches in Hexham, the historical process of people choosing different ways to serve God continues. The outward and visible signs of unity are in specific services, in events such as carol singing around the bandstand, and in the summer holiday club for young children which culminates with another bandstand service. The clergy of the different churches meet regularly. There are weeks of prayer for church unity.

There have been a large number of churches in Hexham. In such a small area as Holy Island the name itself indicates the number of places of worship; we witness a tendency for people to create churches to suit themselves. How else can we see the divisions that have been made at best peacefully and at worst with bloodshed?

The Abbey itself, through its central position and the quality of its building, speaks of the amount of time and money people were prepared to give for the glory of God, although for some this may have been a way of buying themselves into Heaven. From its foundation it followed the Roman Catholic tradition, strongly advocated by Wilfrid at the Synod of Whitby (as opposed to the Celtic tradition), and when the Reformation led to the Dissolution of the Monasteries to fill Henry VIII's coffers, the local church survived as it was the only place fit for worship. It became part of the Church of England, and has remained so ever since.

Nonconformist churches grew out of dissatisfaction with church liturgy and were a reaction against those in society whose wealth and position were thought sufficient to give them power over religion too. Not only in Hexham, but in the surrounding rural and industrial areas, Methodism in its various forms seemed to reach the parts that established Churches failed to. It was a movement born of working people, by them and for them. From here, though, the variety of options that people demanded of the Church and God caused even more splits, which unity movements are now trying to heal, but people have become set in their ways and comfortable in their form of service among like-minded folk.

Today, therefore, the churches that remain, all with reasonably viable congregations and through hiring out facilities to the many clubs and societies in the town, seem set to continue. The Society of Friends (Quakers) is an exception, in that it rents its meeting place for a 10 a.m. Sunday service at the Community Centre in Gilesgate. Their statement of belief is posted in the local library, and I will quote it:

There is something sacred in all people. All people are equal before God. Religion is about the whole of life. In silence we discover a deeper sense of God's presence. True religion leads to a respect for the Earth, and all life. Each person is unique, precious, a child of God.

Churches Together: a Good Friday Procession of Witness.

Quakers locally are consistently the greatest advocates of peace, to be found from the outset opposing the war in Iraq or the spending of billions on the renewal of the Trident weapons system at the expense of using that money to help eradicate some of the conditions that cause such discontent and hatred of the West. Many of us, and I include myself, are at one with them on this, and this is a great unifying factor, just as Churches Together have raised awareness of the importance of eliminating poverty. Clearly there are many issues where Christians and non-Christians can unite in a world that has gone so badly wrong.

Churches that seem to represent so many people would be thought to cover all shades of opinion, but it is only recently that the Evangelical Hexham Community Church was established in a building that went the way of so many redundant churches, at the junction of Battle Bill and Beaumont Street. The Salvation Army is a presence in its Citadel in Market Street, at one with the other churches. The Abbey was taken from the Roman Catholics, but their faith has always been traditionally strong in the North. Many supported the Jacobites in the early eighteenth century. Although they were banned by law from holding office, some managed to do so because they were considered worthy. It is perhaps because of their social and economic position in the town that their faith was overlooked, and they were able to meet illegally, but with consent. Holy Island, for example, had a Mass House where a parish priest either lived or stayed, and then the Catholics moved to what is now the Priest's House in Cockshaw Terrace before making their final move to the church of St Mary's.

What of the Nonconformists? Their places of worship, some used, some redundant and some destroyed are either still there or recorded. We are left with the Trinity Methodist church in Beaumont Street, the United Reformed church (formerly Scots church, 1824), in Hencotes, and the West End Methodist church.

St Mary the Virgin Roman Catholic church (1830).

Hexham Community church.

The churches together provide a lot of space for various activities, and it is the Abbey that has had most problems in making use of it, especially because the nave retains its early twentieth-century pews, rather like seats in a bus but less comfortable. The north and south transepts and the crossing can be filled with comfortable removable seats and has sufficient flexibility for other uses, such as a recent candlelit dinner and a winter fair, the latter drawing in hundreds of people who might not have been in the Abbey before. Unlike the other churches, the Abbey has a national role as a pilgrimage centre and as a listed building, which places a great strain on its time and resources.

All the churches support the Fair Trade movement, and although this is not specifically a Christian movement, many have joined forces to make Hexham a Fair Trade town. This shows that Hexham is not content to be preserved in aspic; neither does it want to be seen as some feudal stronghold.

These churches are all still in use, but a look around the streets will reveal a Primitive Methodist Chapel in Back Street, a converted chapel building opposite the Old Tannery, Holy Island House, the Priest's House in Cockshaw, a chapel converted into houses in Hallstile, and the Ebenezer Chapel at Broadgates, in use from 1790-1869, now used for the sale of electrical goods. For a Baptist presence in Hexham (see Appendix 3).

Chapter 9

Leisure, Entertainment, Sport and Tourism

The mechanisation of factory and domestic industry has freed most people from hard labour and given them more free time. Economic prosperity also gives people the means to enjoy it. The population is more mobile in its search for work and pleasure, so that local and international tourism flourish, aided by the increasing use of private cars and air travel.

Hexham in the twentieth and twenty-first centuries has sought to attract tourists principally because of its appearance and history as a small market town, and because it has such an interesting environment, especially since the establishment of the 'Hadrian's Wall Corridor'. It has also become a good place for commuters to live, with one of the lowest crime rates in the country, schools of quality and many facilities that make life more interesting. As a result, people with fairly substantial incomes are attracted, and bring with them skills and leisure pursuits that can be passed on to the larger community through local clubs, churches and societies. Road and rail links with Newcastle and Carlisle are good. In the mornings and evenings it is obvious that many come into Hexham to work, and others leave.

There is a dichotomy in Hexham's struggle to figure significantly in the tourist trade because it has allowed the spread of industry along the banks of the river, with the latest huge expansion being that of Egger, manufacturing chip-board, whose new gravity-feed hoppers and other buildings dominate the entrance from the east, and welcome visitors with a steady and large emission of steam. There have been some lost planning opportunities, but the end result is a *fait accompli*, for the chip-board plant now employs directly and indirectly about 1,000 people; this in turn brings income, especially via the rates. Modern architecture seldom fits such an ancient town, although as we have seen in the town centre there can be well-planned and sensitive developments.

If the problem of harmonising with the past is not achieved, Hexham's status will be lost. It is probably better now to ignore some of the river bank sprawl already established and concentrate on those areas that have yet to be developed, as well as trying to improve existing eyesores. Tourism will depend on this: the appearance of the town as much as what it offers in the way of entertainment and shopping. Principally, though, Hexham is for the people who live there. As in many other British towns and cities, the car has created some of the biggest problems of access and parking, and the more people who are attracted, the graver these problems become. The town would be infinitely better if traffic were banned from the historic centre, and that prospect raises indignation in some people.

As it is, even with unsightly parking, the town centre remains attractive, interesting, and in many ways continues to improve. Continuous landscaping of the parklands and the preservation and enhancement of old buildings are now priorities, whereas not long ago the battle seemed to have been lost, with some interesting old buildings and archaeological sites having been destroyed. The coming and going of

Egger.

visitors may have been an important part of the town's economy, but towns cannot depend on that for their inner life. Living in a place is made considerably more attractive by having interesting things to do there. There are two factors in leisure provision: one, the money and staff put into it by local authorities, and the other, the enthusiasm of groups and individuals for setting up activities that others can enjoy. Schools are one of the great providers through sports, drama, music and other activities, and much of the best work is done out of school hours, led by those who believe in its importance and are prepared to give time to it.

The reputation of a school for sport and the arts may rise and fall according to who is leading it and their interests. For example, there has been a switch from improvised drama, where the emphasis was on the children creating a play through exploring ideas, to the set-piece musical, more regimented and adult-led. There continue to be exceptions to this trend; for example, Hexham Middle School has produced many original dramas, incorporating dance and music, based on ideas clearly stemming from the pupils and involving vast numbers in the productions. There was a time when Northumberland teachers of drama met regularly and held courses in which they explored together the same kind of situations that they worked out with their pupils. To some extent the coming of the National Curriculum stifled this activity with the bureaucratic demands on teachers' time. One cannot 'test' drama, music and art in the same way that one tests literacy and numeracy. Yet drama is one of the greatest devices for the exploration of ideas and vocabulary that one can wish for. The set school play is much easier to stage, by selecting the most able to perform in it. Involving everyone requires a different approach and is more demanding. Attendance at school dramatic productions of whatever kind is always guaranteed to be healthy, and considerable talent is always on show.

There is a strong tradition of musicianship in some Hexham families, where children can learn to be skilled performers without very much outside help. This reveals itself in many local choirs and orchestras. Hexham Abbey, a dominant building, has one of the finest organs in the country, one choir that still traditionally remains male but also a girls' choir and a Chamber Choir that performs on special occasions. There is high-quality music, week in, week out at regular services including Wednesday and

Festival
performers.

Thursday evensong. Many parents regard these choirs as one of the best musical educations for their children, and there is a constant stream of young people who develop skills as organists and choristers. The Abbey hosts some very high-quality school performances, notably those of Queen Elizabeth High School, which has a special status as a centre of excellence for the arts. Add all this to other groups in the town, and it makes an impressive list.

Hexham Abbey has had its tradition of Church music recorded from Anglian times from Acca onwards; he was responsible for bringing Church music from the Continent, but it could not have reached today's heights. The annual Hexham Abbey Festival reached number fifty-five in 2007, now variously funded, with a local committee and a well-established national reputation. It has moved forward to include exciting street theatre and includes in its programme a strong international music element. It balances local programmes with groups of wider fame, having included, for example, the King's Singers, Tenebrae, and the Cardinall's Musick for the final Candlelight Concert. It is not confined to the Abbey building: the 2006 programme included at the Queen's Hall the Kintamarni Saxophone Quartet (including one local girl), Stacey Kent and the Jim Tomlinson Quartet (with Jim also from Hexham). In the Abbey the same week were the Festival Chorus and Orchestra, drawn from all over the area, and showing how many members of choirs join in to share their talents: Antiphon, a chamber choir based in the Tyne valley and set up in 2000 to specialise in the singing of music from the English and European Renaissance, Apu, a group of Peruvian brothers who set up home in the North East and have lived here for seventeen years, and in the same year came Gamelan Naga Mas, a performance of traditional and contemporary south-eastern Asian music by a group that links Glasgow with Indonesia.

Thus the festival combines a wide range of traditions of music and performance. Recently, too, there has been the inclusion of drama and poetry reading in the programme, with jazz and other performances in the streets of Hexham.

The Abbey is a very busy place, with its services, bell-ringing, visitors, pilgrims, concerts and its increasing use by schools. This makes it difficult to rehearse in! Yet there has to be time for quietness, for reflection. From December to January the Abbey housed Rosie Musgrave's sculpture, 'Tsunami Noni',

In rehearsal: the Spindlestone Dragon and prince at the top of the night stair.

which is being shown in many holy places in England, and the sculptress was impressed with how she could for a while sit in the north transept in peace for a long time with her creation, as winter sunlight slanted through the long lancet windows.

The Abbey is an ideal place for so many different kinds of events; as my poem suggests, viewing it by candlelight whilst listening to superb music is one of the great experiences of life. It changes as the sunlight moves at different times of year, illuminating different parts individually. Its shape, although causing producers to think very carefully about sight lines and acoustics, offers exciting possibilities for the use of the building. To illustrate this, I draw on my own experience, for I have produced many events and taken part in others over the past thirty years here. I used to get 'The Abbey People' together for productions of plays. The idea was to involve anyone interested, young and old, irrespective of their experience. On one occasion visitors to the Abbey would have been amazed to find a huge dragon's head waiting in the north aisle to be attached to its 30ft-long body on the parapet at the top of the night stair.

The story was based on the Spindlestone Dragon legend, a good old-fashioned legend of witchcraft, a jealous stepmother, good-versus-evil that filled the Abbey with witches and warlocks (including the Rector's wife), princes, kings, princesses, villagers, maypole dancers (from a local First School), the Abbey Choir and other musicians, and some dramatic sound and lighting effects. This had previously been performed in a different version by pupils from local schools in the Queen's Hall as a festival production, one of three major productions within the festival at different times, including the home-grown *The Judgement of Solomon* and *Starflight Genesis*. All three plays were also performed by different groups of various children on BBC Radio Newcastle, so there was a high standard demanded of them.

Also performed in the Abbey was T.S. Eliot's *Murder in the Cathedral*, again by people whose experience of theatre was varied. The two principals, who shared the leading role of Becket on different nights, had not done this sort of thing before. I prefer working with non-professional actors. One of the most satisfying moments in the play was where the audience, sitting in the north transept and crossing,

Young people from local schools recording *Starflight Genesis* at BBC Radio Newcastle following a Hexham Abbey Festival performance in The Queen's Hall.

Folkworks.

could see Becket being robed for his sermon as the Abbey Choir sang a *Dies Irae,* in clothes suggested by the archivist from Canterbury Cathedral (who attended the performance). He made his way in procession to the pulpit at the side of the audience while the cast moved to engulf everyone with lighted candles, and preached a sermon that is one of Mr Eliot's finest pieces of writing. This was where the building, history, aspiration and humanity came together.

The last production that I arranged there was called *Shepherds, Rogues and Angels*, based on medieval themes such as *Everyman*, The Wakefield Cycle's *Second Shepherd's Play*, and Chaucer's *The Pardoner's Tale*. This time the audience faced north to a platform built at the end of the north transept, and a group of young musicians, trained by a teacher and well-known jazz pianist, the late Ken Morrell, who formed an Elizabethan-type instrumental ensemble from Corbridge Middle School, with the Abbey men's choir providing plainsong.

Perhaps one of the finest dramas that I have experienced in the Abbey was *Son of Man*, performed by Queen Elizabeth High School. Beginning with a formidable and threatening young man at the west door in full Roman armour, moving to many locations in the Abbey, taking the audience along with the story metaphorically and literally, the message of Jesus was delivered under the tower crossing as the audience and cast held hands around him in a circle. It was brilliantly conceived and totally convincing.

Finally, for a performance of Buxtehude's *Membra Jesu Nostri*, the local chamber group, 'Antiphon', asked me to write and read poetry based upon the sections of the Mass that dealt with the parts of Christ's body and with what we might associate them, to provide reflections on the theme and to make breaks in the music for contrast. Again, the use of candles as the main illumination created an incredible atmosphere to heighten the music and words, and what they meant.

For example:

It is the eyes that mirror most our souls.
Glazed false serenity of addict's dazed dilation
In choosing an escape that only makes things worse.
Eyes easily angered leap to life when raw nerves fire.
Eyes, soft and warm surge sympathy from wells of deep commitment and content.
Lovers lock lives and passion eye to eye.
Ashamed, our eyes slide sideways to an empty space.

We thus betray an inner life or open up a terrifying emptiness inside.
The body's fountainhead, the brain,
More complex than anything invented by itself
Controls our feelings and our thoughts.
No matter how the face prepares itself
Or is prepared cosmetically
Truth pushes through to show us and our neighbours what we are.

Although there were moments of fun in many of these productions, the principal aim was serious. There is plenty of opportunity for comedy and pantomime, as we see in so many local productions.

In the town, the Theatre Club and Hexham Amateur Stage Society are based at the Queen's Hall and perform there to large audiences. The same venue draws in crowds too for school productions and those of the Young Farmers. The library can be a venue for anthologies of music and words, such as *Things That Go Bump in the Night* or *Birds, Beasts and Flowers*, or for talks; the café can host jazz, rock and comedy shows. Churches and church halls also host major performances, for there are many choirs to take up the spaces.

All in all, there is an incredible amount going on in the town, and scope for extending these activities. One increasingly important group, again based on the Queen's Hall, is the Theatre Sans Frontières, which tours with productions in foreign languages, making them accessible to a wide audience.

There is a Hexham Abbey Festival Chorus, Hexham Male Voice Choir, and Hexham Orpheus Choir, and a Tyneside orchestra, all producing concerts of quality. Outside performing artists arrive through the Hexham and District Music Society and Friends of Abbey Music.

A scene from *Shepherds, Rogues and Angels* by 'The Abbey People' in the north transept.

Folkworks in the Tap and Spile.

One of the most significant changes in the provision of entertainment has been the arrival of Folkworks. This is largely for young people to play traditional music, and the impetus has again come from people with mission and the skill to follow a vision. On some weekends the town centre and its streets are alive with groups of young people, not all local, playing a variety of instruments in a variety of styles, from fiddles to steel drums. There is a growing overseas presence, especially with links forged with Scandinavia. Adults are there too and the pubs receive groups of musicians who give impromptu concerts just for the fun of it.

An addition to the programme of events on the Sele and Abbey Grounds has been Selefest, which caters for far from traditional groups of young musicians, and this, along with rock groups that

Iain Duncan, Frosts and Fires
Visual Art at Queen's Hall, Hexham - Gallery Two - Saturday, 2 December to Saturday, 22 January, 2007

'Frosts and Fires' in the Queen's Hall. (© Iain Duncan)

sometimes perform at the Hexham Carnival, has cast the music net wider. Poor performances do not pass unnoticed. *The Hexham Courant* has its group of reviewers in addition to its own reporters and they do not suffer the failures of professional groups gladly, but are kinder to local amateur performances. The newspaper gives plenty of notice about productions and provides many photographs.

Arts and crafts are not confined to the town, as there is a network of artists and craftspeople throughout Tynedale. Each year they now arrange an 'Art Tour', inviting people to their studios. The Queen's Hall, Moothall and Abbey have frequent exhibitions of local and national work, mostly of high quality. There is a high standard of embroidery, as visitors to the Abbey will witness, and it is amazing how many people are involved in their homes too. There has been growing interest in what digital imaging can produce; an example of the work of Iain Duncan, 'Frosts and Fires' (above), was part of a very successful exhibition.

Many of these artists give others the benefit of their experience through teaching, such as Birtley Aris, whose County Council courses at Ford Castle attracted people from all over Britain, and whose commissioned paintings of Durham Cathedral, Hexham Abbey, landscapes and jazz have reached a wide audience.

Sports are catered for in schools, where the key element is the enthusiasm and skill of individual members of staff and the time they are prepared to give. Outside schools there are many clubs. A glimpse at *The Hexham Courant's* Tynedale Community Guide 2006/7 may come as a surprise. In Hexham alone there is provision for athletics, badminton, basketball, bowling (indoor and outdoor), canoeing, football, golf, hockey, judo, karate, martial arts, netball, riding, rugby union, swimming, volleyball, and walking.

The success of such activities depends on both individual and corporate initiatives, and the funding of facilities is a key factor. A focus of such activity is at the Wentworth Leisure Centre, which is being extended to include a 25-metre, 6-lane swimming pool, a large fitness gym and associated facilities. The local council's role is to support initiatives that lead to more people being involved in sport.

Clubs and Societies

Again, reading a document like this reveals just how many activities are going on. There is a 'Torch' Open Recreation Centre for the Handicapped, a Beekeepers' Association, a branch of the British Sugarcraft Guild, a Hexham and District Flower Club, the Hexham Decorative and Fine Arts Society, the Hexham and District Flower Club, the Hexham and District Philatelic Society, the Local History Society, the Photographic Society, Probus Club, Tangent Club, the Historic Hexham Trust, Hexham Homing Pigeon Society, Inner Wheel, Ladies' Circles, National Trust Tyne Valley Association, the Northumberland and Durham Family History Society, Rotary Clubs, Royal Air Force Association, a Town Twinning Association, Women's Institute, the Hexham Business Forum and the Hexham Guild of Guides.

There are many clubs that further the interests of dance: Ballet, Hexham Country Dance Club, Hexham Folk Dance Club, and Scottish Country Dancing. Not only is there a *Talking Newspaper and Magazine for the Blind*, but also there is, uniquely, an arts and crafts group for blind and visually impaired people, meeting fortnightly. There is a 'Yew Tree' project in operation, with a book prefaced by David Bellamy now published. The Northumberland Cancer Support group is well-established in Hexham. There is a Youth Initiative Club based on the Community Centre, Scout groups and Girl Guides, Brownies and Rainbows.

One of the most important environmental groups in Hexham is the Civic Society, which acts as a watch dog on developments in the town, and arranges for speakers to come and put their point of view. It has an excellent newsletter which, along with *The Hexham Courant*, enables us to keep an eye on developments so that at least we know what is going on; the first condition of a democracy.

Last, but by no means least, are provisions for adult education, in which the Queen Elizabeth High School continues to provide many courses, including a youth theatre, and where the Gatehouse is an Open Learning Centre. Recently Newcastle College has expanded its provision in Hexham; there is a flourishing Tynedale U3A and a Workers' Educational Association. There is North East Chamber of Commerce training, and a Training Agency.

Appendix 1

The Archaeology of the Abbey

The main text in chapter one illustrates the east cloister wall. What follows is more detail brought to light by recent archaeological research and by the reassessment of past reports.

The excavation showed that this cloister wall actually cut into earlier, well-defined deposits, including mortar that was part of a floor and a shallow post hole surrounded by small and large stones where a wooden post had stood for a 'comparatively long time', possibly part of a framed structure, inside a building, possibly supporting an upper floor. The bones of about twenty-seven people had been disturbed and reburied there in a charnel pit in the thirteenth century, so part of the site may have been a burial ground. There were the remains of a north-south wall running through what is now the shop, which is known to continue inside the south transept, under the floor. The Saxon crypt had already been excavated and made safe in 1978. When all reports on previous investigations are put together, it amounts to a very complex series of buildings that can now only be seen on plans.

It seems that Wilfrid's church had a small rectangular chancel above the crypt, a long narrow rectangular nave about the same size as the churches at Jarrow and Monkwearmouth, perhaps with an aisle to the south slightly larger than that to the north. Acca, the bishop who is reputed to have brought a fine musical tradition to the church, is reported to have built a 'portico', a kind of foyer entrance to the west.

The plans show that the pre-Augustinian buildings (mid-twelfth-century) near the Chapter House were in slightly different places from later ones. For example, the eastern cloister wall was recorded in part to the west of the present one. The rest of the buildings, the Norman (or 'Romanesque') church to which it was attached, lay on the present nave line, with a small transept to the north and a larger one to the south, the east and west walls of which extended south, one outside and one inside what is now the gift shop. A passage from the cloisters east, like the Slype today further south, may have gone through from cloisters to the east. The plans show this.

Of great interest to archaeologists is where this church ended in the east. A rounded end ('apsidal') was found that marked such an end, then the remains of another beyond that; one is presumed to belong to the Saxon chapel of St Peter, and the other to the end of the Norman church. You will see that after this rounded end there is a large chancel running east, which was rebuilt in the nineteenth century. Did anything lie in that space before? The apsidal end of the older building suggests that it might have been a chapel. It had pre-Conquest burials around it, which could have been disturbed in its building, and the inside of the chapel used for important people. Could one have been for the pre-Viking burial of a king called Aelfwold (788)? Buildings with important relics attract pilgrims and donations, and rich people like to claim the sanctity of being buried close to them – in which case the chapel with an apsidal end could have been a repository for the remains of important people.

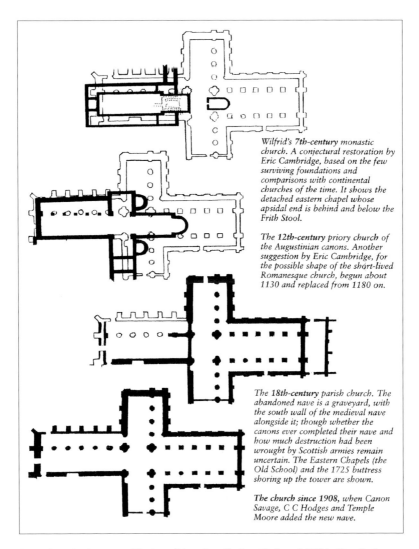

*Wilfrid's **7th-century** monastic church. A conjectural restoration by Eric Cambridge, based on the few surviving foundations and comparisons with continental churches of the time. It shows the detached eastern chapel whose apsidal end is behind and below the Frith Stool.*

*The **12th-century** priory church of the Augustinian canons. Another suggestion by Eric Cambridge, for the possible shape of the short-lived Romanesque church, begun about 1130 and replaced from 1180 on.*

*The **18th-century** parish church. The abandoned nave is a graveyard, with the south wall of the medieval nave alongside it; though whether the canons ever completed their nave and how much destruction had been wrought by Scottish armies remain uncertain. The Eastern Chapels (the Old School) and the 1725 buttress shoring up the tower are shown.*

***The church since 1908**, when Canon Savage, C C Hodges and Temple Moore added the new nave.*

Plans of the development of Hexham Abbey, from *Hexham Heritage* (1999) by Tom Corfe, with his permission, produced for the Hexham Civic Society in 1999.

The Term 'Abbey'

In the text the 'Abbey' has also been referred to as 'Wilfrid's church', 'Wilfrid's cathedral', 'The Priory' and 'monastery'. Today its title is 'Hexham Abbey: the Priory and Parish church of St Andrew', because it had monks living there (which is the same as a monastery when it is for men only). It is correct to call it a Priory, for it was a small establishment for canons who lived and worked there.

Under Wilfrid and other bishops it was a cathedral, their 'seat', the centre of administration of the diocese, where the bishop's *cathedra* (seat) was. This survives literally as the 'Frith stool' in the chancel. It ceased to be a cathedral *c*. AD 821.

Under Wilfrid, the Benedictine monks obeyed the law of St Benedict. After the Norman Conquest it followed the rule of Augustine, so we have Augustinian canons living there.

In the eighteenth century any old building linked with the church was known as an Abbey (thus Jane Austen's *Northanger Abbey*). The Beaumont family who owned it were happy to call it that; their home was the Abbey and their garden the Abbey Grounds.

Baptists in Hexham

Baptists make only a brief appearance in Hexham. Professor Roger Howell's article in *Archaeologia Aeliana* explores in depth an event or incident that has not often been mentioned in accounts of Hexham's history that occurred on 4 June 1653. A man who was believed to be a Jewish rabbi was baptised in the River Tyne by total immersion after his supposed conversion, but before the end of the month was proved to be an impostor. It was not just the embarrassment of the Church having had the wool pulled over its eyes that resulted from this, but also the divisions caused between the congregations of Hexham and Newcastle that make it such an interesting story. These were the main centres of the Baptist Church established in the North East after the English Civil War. That, in Newcastle, was probably due to the presence of the army, but the prime mover in Hexham was not an army man; Thomas Tillam, from Cheshire originally, came to Hexham in 1651 and settled there as a 'Lecturer', a post established in 1625 by the Mercers to provide people with proper guidance through preaching.

How the Baptist movement began in the area is not clear, but when he arrived, Thomas described the church as a wonderful appearance of God 'in this dark corner'. His background is obscure, too, although at some time he had been a Roman Catholic. He successfully founded a 'Particular' Baptist congregation in Hexham when he baptised eleven men and five women, and his wife was added to the number. By 1654 there were forty-five men and thirty-eight women in the congregation, which speaks well of Tillam's vigour and evangelism. The success of the new church, though, produced a counter-reaction from conservatives who found the movement aggressive and anarchic. Of particular concern was the doctrine of baptism, but other criticism included charges such as blasphemy. The main church in Newcastle disagreed with that of Hexham, involving personality clashes of the leaders. Tillam, for example, saw that a full-time minister needed full-time payment, and he saw himself as a pastor. This is the background to the 'false Jew' episode.

The man at the centre was Thomas Horsley, who told the commander of the ship that had brought him from Hamburg that he was a Newcastle man, and that he was part of a Jesuit plot to seduce the English. In Newcastle he set up the story that he was a Jewish rabbi born in Munster who could speak eight languages, had studied philosophy, now doubted his faith, and had 'found Christ' through the Baptists.

Tillam was convinced of this, though many were sceptical. Perhaps the conversion of a Jew became for him the ultimate triumph of his mission. So 'Joseph Ben Israel' was baptised. The suspicions of the Newcastle Baptists of this man who spoke perfect dialect English and who was so familiar with England led to a formal hearing, held in the city in the presence of the mayor and other officials. The 'Jew' then confessed that he was Thomas Ramsey, born in London of Scottish parents. He had studied at Edinburgh and Glasgow, travelled to Germany and then to Rome, training with the Dominicans and at a Jesuit college to counter heresy in England.

Tillam and his flock accepted that they had been duped, and attributed the unmasking of Ramsay to the mercy of God rather than to the Newcastle clergy. Because there were many papists in the Hexham area, he blamed them.

Ramsay offered to turn informer, but we hear no more of him; all this had a bad effect on the Hexham church as the rifts already there widened: doctrinal, personal and political. Tillam had to go, but he continued his colourful career elsewhere.

Bibliography

There is no detailed, comprehensive history of Hexham. There are many accounts of various aspects of this history, some written many years ago, and many continue to be written. My account brings some of these sources to the fore, but remains a brief history and guide. The Abbey has particularly had considerable attention paid to its story, including its place in the early history of the Christian church, but it is only recently that other buildings and themes are receiving their due. There is also increasing interest in more recent history, as this bibliography demonstrates, much of it the result of some impressive academic research. Hexham Local History Society publications (HLHS) are among the most frequent.

Beckensall, S. 1991. *Hexham: History Beneath Our Feet* (Peter Robson, Hexham)

Beckensall, S. 2002. *Northumberland: The Power of Place* (Tempus)

Beckensall, S. 2005. *Northumberland: Shadows of the Past* (Tempus)

Cambridge, E. and Williams, A.J.T. 1995. *Hexham Abbey: A review of recent work and its implications* (AA 5th series, XXIII, 51-138)

Chapman, J. (no date) *A Walk Back in Time: A Guide to Hexham* (Glen Graphics)

Charlesworth, D. 1952. *The Battle of Hexham, 1464* (AA 4th series XXX 57-68)

Charlton, M. 1987. *Old Hexham* (Peter Robson Print)

Corfe, T. 1999. *Hexham Heritage* (Hexham Civic Society)

Corfe, T. 2004. *Riot* (Hexham Community Partnership)

Corfe, T. (Ed). 2006. *Hexham Lives* (Occasional publication No. 7 HLHS)

Grint, A. I. 2006. *The Faith and the Fire Within, In memory of the men of Hexham who fell in the Great War* (Ergo Press, Hexham)

Hinds, A.B. 1896. *A History of Northumberland, Vol. III, Hexhamshire. Part 1* (A. Reid, Newcastle)

Hodges, C.C. 1888. *Ecclesia Hagustaldensis: the Abbey of St Andrew, Hexham* (private)

Hodges, C.C. and Gibson, J. 1919. *Hexham and its Abbey* (Batsford)

Hoole, K. (Ed.) 1967. *Thomlinson's North East Railway Book* (David and Charles)

Howell, R. 1986. *Conflict and controversy in the early Baptist movement in Northumberland: Thomas Tillam, Paul Hobson and the False Jew of Hexham* (Archaeologia Aeliana 5th Series XIV 81-99)

Jennings, D. 2002. *Finding Out* (HLHS). (This is a useful guide to sources, including stored archival material, names and addresses of people with expertise, books and articles. These include both the local and broader picture so that Hexham can be seen in its context of national history.)

Jennings, D., Corfe, T., Rossiter, A., Sobell, L. 2005. *The Heart of all England: Hexham's Story in Original Documents* (Occasional publication No. 5 HLHS)

Kirby, D.P. (Ed.) 1974. *Saint Wilfrid at Hexham* (Oriel Press)

Kristensen, H. and Dallison, C. 2006. *Hexham Remembered: An Illustrated Glimpse into Hexham's Past* (Wagtail Press)

Jennings, R.A. 1996. *School Board for Hexham* (HH. 6)

Jennings, D. et al. 2005. *The Heart of all England: Hexham's Story in Original Documents* (Occasional publication No. 5 HLHS)

Jennings, D. *Hexham 1854-1939. Local Government in a Market Town* (Occasional publication No. 6 HLHS)

Linsley, S.M. 1994. *Tyne Crossings at Hexham up to 1795* (AA 5th series. XXII 235-253)

Mais, S.P.M. 1935. *England's Pleasaunce* (Hutchinson and Co.)

Maxwell, H. 1913 (trans.). *The Chronicle of Lanercost 1272-1346* (James Mackenzie and Sons, Glasgow)

Morton, K. 1987. *Old Hexham* (Peter Robson Print, Hexham)

Parson, W. and White, W. 1827. *History, Directory and Gazetteer of the Counties of Durham and Northumberland Vol. 1* (White and Co., Newcastle)

Pevsner, N. 1992. *The Buildings of England: Northumberland* (Penguin)

Rawlinson, R. 1853. *Report to the General Board of Health etc* (HMSO, London)

Reprints of rare tracts. 1899. (Lansdown MSS, British Library, reprinted by M.A. Richardson, Newcastle)

Ryder, P. 1994. *The Two Towers of Hexham* (*Archaeologia Aeliana*, 5th Series, XXII)

Sadler, D. forthcoming. *The Battle of Hexham* (Ergo Press, Hexham)

Sharp, C.S. 1824. *Original Account of the Riot at Hexham, by an officer of the North Yorks Militia* (*The Newcastle Magazine*, pp. 297-9)

Totton, W. 1761. *On the Important Duty of Subjection to the Civil Powers etc* (Thompson, Richardson, Featherstone: Newcastle, London and Hexham)

Warn, C.R. 1978. *Buses in Northumberland and Durham. Part 1 1900-1930* (F. Graham, Newcastle)

Wright, A.B. 1823. *An Essay towards the Study of Hexham* (W. Davison, Alnwick)

Documents held in the Northumberland Record Office:
Relating to Hexham Workhouse (NRO 3589). A copy is available in the Brough Collection, Hexham Library, 362.58094288.

In the Old Gaol, there is a very important, extensive collection of local research material donated by David Jennings. The storage facilities there are of great importance, and researchers are encouraged to add material to it for posterity.

The Hexham Historian

1. 1991. Including: 'Hexham Excavations 1990' (Beckensall, S.), 'Dr Joseph Parker' (Stokoe, D.), 'St Mary's Chare' (Corfe, T.), 'The Gentleman's Magazine' (Chapman, J.), 'How Hexham Got its Name' (Corfe, T.)
2. 1992. Including: 'Two Wells' (Beckensall, S.), 'Sundials Around Hexham' (Ransom, P.), 'The Dating of High Shield' (Chapman, J.), 'A day in the life of the Borough Court' (Jackman, J.)
3. 1993. Including: 'Excavations at Hexham Abbey' (Ryder, P.), 'Earliest Northumbria' (Corfe, T.), 'The Inspeximus of 1298' (Wilson, A.), 'Bridging the Tyne' (Linsley, S.)

4. 1994. 'Cockshaw' (a team effort)

5. 1995. Including: 'The Place Name Hexham' (Watts, V.), 'Hexham after the Vikings' (Rollason, D.), 'The Medieval Topography of Hexham' (Corfe, T.), 'The growth of Hexham in the 1890s' (Higgins, R.), 'Regional Government Headquarters, Hexham' (Short, M.)

6. 1996. Including: 'The Government of Hexham in the 17th Century' (Rossiter, A.), 'A School Board for Hexham' (Jennings, R.)

7. 1997. 'Before Wilfrid' (Ed. Corfe, T.)

8. 1998. Including: 'The Queen and the Robber' (Corfe, T.), 'Joseph Catherall of *The Hexham Courant*' (Jennings, R.), 'Two (1872 and 1935) Contemporary Accounts of Poor Housing in Hexham' (Jennings, D.)

9. 1999. 'From Grammar School to High School, 1599-1999' (Ed. Jennings, D., Rossiter, A.)

10. 2000. Including: 'A Decade of Archaeology in Hexham' (Beckensall, S. and Ryder, P.), 'Hexham Cinemas' (Johnson, G. and Jennings, D.) 'Life in a Hexham Street: Priestpopple, Cattle Market and Battle Hill' (Dallison, M.), 'Economic and Social Indicators for Hexham: an Analysis of the 1851 and 1891 Census' (Jennings, D.)

11. 2001. Including: 'The End of Hexham Priory' (Harvey, M.), 'The Origins of the Hexham Hydro' (Strom, K.), 'Memoirs of Hexham Hydro' (Bradley, C.), 'Restoration of the Abbey: Savage versus Lockhart' (Jennings, D.)

12. 2002. Including: 'The Wars of the Roses in Northumberland 1461-64' (Corfe, T.), 'Hexham Mechanics' Literary and Scientific Institution' (Jenkins, B.), 'Hexham Primitive Methodist Church' (Payne, E.), 'The 1853 Cholera Outbreak in Hexham' (Jennings, D.), 'Death in Hexham in the Late 16th and 17th Centuries' (Rossiter, A.), 'Death in the Tyne Valley' (Beckensall, S)

13. 2003. Including: 'The Hospital of St Giles at Hexham' (Gardner-Medwin, D.), 'Eilaf's Vision' (Corfe, T.), 'Border Warfare and Hexhamshire in the Later Middle Ages' (Goodman, A.), '1841 and a Revolution in Hexham's Townscape' (Jennings, D.)

14. 2004. Including: 'Two Militia Lists (1762 and 1803) for Hexham' (Higgins, R. and Jennings, D.), 'The Society of Shoemakers' (Jennings, D.), 'Hexham Hydro – A Chronological History' (Dalllison, C. and Jennings, D.), 'Soldiers Who Died in the Great War' (Grint, A.)

15. 2005. Including: 'The Hagustaldian Church' (Corfe, T.), 'A Load of Old Cobblers' (Rossiter, A.), 'The Great Flood of 1771 in Hexham' (Jennings, D.), 'Two Hexham Iron Works' (Jennings, D.), 'Only Fools and Horses' (Grint, A.)

16. 2006. Including: 'Clock and Watchmakers of Hexham' (Higgins, R.), 'How Many Rioters Were There?' (Jennings, D.), 'The History of a House' (Higgins, R.), 'Suffragettes in Hexham' (Rossiter, A.), 'Pattinsons of Hexham – and Beyond' (Baker, H.)

In addition to *The Hexham Historian*, the Society produces a newsletter more frequently, and this often has additional pieces of local research included.

Postscript

The life of an active town is ever-changing. In the short time that this book has been in the hands of the Tempus editor, the old established firm of Robb's went into liquidation through its owners, despite its being viable. The staff have been on a roller-coaster of insecurity, and were relieved when it was thought that a new buyer had been found. This may prove illusory. We all hope not.

The rapid expansion of the Egger chipboard factory, as the most modern of its kind, has aroused hostility among some for the way it dominates the approaches to Hexham from the east, whereas others weigh this up against some financial benefit to the town and its workers.

Hexham is earmarked for the site of a new Town Hall in spite of whether it becomes part of a single unitary county body or of two. A new purpose-built hall which accommodates all its departments will free some very valuable and attractive premises.

The construction of the new six-lane swimming pool at the Wentworth Leisure Centre is going well, and its completion will free yet another historic building, once a wool factory.

Tesco is well established and successful, but the Co-op is earmarked for closure (along with one of the biggest car-park spaces in the town centre).

Little victories against the threat of adverse planning applications have been celebrated; a line of flowering trees outside the police station has been saved from felling to make way for an enlarged car park there, thanks to very strong local opinion and action.

The greatest architectural triumph has been the conversion of the seventeenth-century George and Dragon Inn from decayed and drab premises abutting the old Priory wall to a superb open space for cafés and shops. Part of its front, looking onto St Mary's Chare, has been cleaned of its concrete facing to reveal irregular millstone grit cobbles of great charm and character, and its attics and gables have been tastefully restored. One hopes that the owner will now extend this work to the adjoining building.

Work on the Cockshaw Burn drainage has resulted in brilliant use of stone walling to accompany the culverting, and buildings at the Tyne end are being renovated and rebuilt. Again, this has been done with great skill and concern for the historic environment and has further transformed the once-derelict industrial area.Rail links to Newcastle and Carlisle are apparently saved, and may be increased. Talk about a new bus station continues.

Finally, in May Hexham became again the centre of a folk gathering, with mainly enthusiastic and skilled young people, taking over streets, parkland and premises in a way that was sheer delight for them, the residents and tourists. Culturally, Hexham continues to be on a high with the Abbey Festival beginning on 28 September and a BBC *Songs of Praise* feature planned for the autumn.

Index